THEY CAME FROM POLAND

THEY CAME
FROM POLAND

The Stories of Famous Polish-Americans

LAURA PILARSKI

ILLUSTRATED

DODD, MEAD & COMPANY

NEW YORK

Library of Congress Catalog Card Number: 69-17599
Printed in the United States of America
by The Haddon Craftsmen, Inc., Scranton, Penna.

In grateful tribute to my parents
who also
came from Poland

Contents

Illustrations

PRONUNCIATION OF POLISH NAMES

On American soil, Polish names have taken on an English pronunciation partly because sounds in the Polish language are not so easily spoken. But the task is not so difficult if some simple rules are remembered. Try, at least, to pronounce the famous names encountered in this book by keeping in mind:

j, is always pronounced like y
i, like ee
w, like the English v
u, like oo
cz, like the Englsh ch, as in child
sz, like sh, as in shall
rz, very much like the French j, as in jardin
szcz, like stch
ch, nearly like h
g, is spoken hard, like g in get

The Poles Come to Settle

"Although pilgrims in a foreign land, with nothing
but the sad recollection of the past and hopes for
the future, we wish to live a life of active industry
and become useful to the land of our adoption."

THEY CAME in the stuffy holds of steamers slowly
moving across the Atlantic, a huddled mass of passengers wedged into every measurable inch of steerage
space. Poor and untutored, rumpled-looking and sea-
sick, they were, for the most part, simple farm folk
departed from the families, the villages, the soil, the
traditions they knew and loved. They carried their
small wealth with them in forlorn bundles. They
looked miserably cramped, yet they were uncomplain-
ing. Their words, songs, and prayers poured forth in
familiar Slavic syllables, hovering in the dank quarters
like comforting incense.

These were the Polish immigrants flocking to Amer-

1

ica just before and after the turn of the century. Some were only in their teens and many had never before set foot beyond their own hamlets. They stemmed from a land of proud history and from a people known for a strong patriotism and passionate attachment to their native earth. Why were they embarked on an awesome and adventurous journey to a faraway country foreign to them? They were escaping twin evils of poverty and oppression.

Poland, at this time, was not to be found on the map of the world; it had been sliced up completely by the end of the 1700's by Prussia, Russia, and Austria and these occupying powers had ruled the partitioned land for more than a century. This subjugation had been effected during a period of internal strife and dwindled strength in a nation which had ranked as a great power of Europe. Different brave but abortive insurrections were launched by the Poles to dislodge foreign rule, but to no avail. The pattern of economic exploitation, political suppression, and cultural constraint not only continued, but deepened. Great masses of poor Poles chose to leave "the old country" to seek a future in a young land that promised them what they most lacked: Opportunity, freedom, prosperity.

What were these newcomers, these lowliest of passengers traveling steerage class, to accomplish in the nation they elected to adopt as their own? They, and millions like them—some who came before and others afterward, representing a multitude of nations and all races—produced what we can only call the miracle of America.

Their achievement outshone even the most imaginative speculation. They pushed the physical and economic growth of their adopted country to unprecedented boundaries and shaped an even more remarkable kind of richness—the enduring richness of the United States as a celebrated "Nation of Immigrants," a mosaic of different faces, different cultures, different races, different lands. Significantly, this was a mosaic cemented not only through success but in suffering, heartbreak, failure, and setback, as well. Surely, the transplanted Polish peasants, struggling at factory jobs, bewildered with the new language and confused by social customs, must have wondered, at times, why they had left old ills for so many new difficulties. No doubt, they took little comfort in their homey peasant dialogue that went like this: "What news?" . . . "Nothing interesting, just old misery." . . . "Well, better old than new."

Yet, while possibly disheartened by new distress, the immigrants—whether Polish, German, Italian, Greek, Irish, or another nationality—never felt themselves defeated. For them, opportunity and hope survived all adversity and they persisted by sheer will and stubborn purpose in their goal of making a better life.

Although Polish life in the United States is a continuous recent history of three, or maybe four, generations, the role of individual immigrants from Poland began much earlier than popularly supposed.

The first Poles actually set foot on American soil before the Mayflower landed. These settlers—a hardy handful—landed at Jamestown in 1608 aboard the supply ship, *Mary and Margaret*. They came as specialists in industry, charged with establishing shops for the manufacture of glass, tar, pitch, and soap ashes. In the earliest records, they are referred to as "Polonians," "Polackers," or "Polanders."

From the outset, they won notice as workers and fighters. Captain John Smith, intrepid leader of the ill-fated Virginia colony which went down in history as the first permanent English settlement in America, excluded the "Polonians" from the scornful "vagabond gentlemen" epithet with which he tagged some settlers. In 1609, Poles were credited with saving Captain Smith's life during the course of an Indian ambush. It was later that the strong-willed newcomers staged what was probably the earliest demonstration on American soil for civil rights.

The year was 1619. The Poles living in Virginia staged a sit-down; they refused to continue on their jobs. The reason? They had not been granted the same voting and representation privileges as afforded settlers of English descent. They demanded equal civil rights.

Their collective protest traveled to London to arbitration there by the Virginia Company and, in the end, they won. Under the terms of settlement, the Poles were enfranchised and "made as free as any inhabitant . . ." Subsequently, a laconic note in Virginia annals proclaimed: "The Polackers are returned to their work." This early blow for civil liberty came at a time when the entire population of Poles on the North American continent numbered possibly fifty in all.

Names unmistakedly Polish cropped up at different places in the colonies and identified settlers who were soldiers, farmers, traders, frontiersmen, teachers. But early immigration never assumed any substantial proportions, mostly because residents of Poland were engaged in a series of defensive wars and because they felt so attached to soil and country. Invasion by Sweden, entanglements in the Ukraine, wars with Russia and Turkey—all were events which occupied and weakened Poland, leaving the country, ruled by kings, exhausted and spent in the seventeenth and eighteenth centuries.

Doubtless, the first wayfarers from Poland were lured, above all, by the beckoning spirit of adventure and an aroused curiosity about a land already described in the sixteenth century as an "heroic paradise." There even is a claim, which must be put down as legend, that a seafaring Pole called Jan of Kolno, in the service of

the king of Denmark, touched the shores of America
sixteen years before Columbus accomplished the feat.

It is estimated that more than one hundred Poles
were mustered on colonial soil to fight in the American
army from 1775 to 1783 during the Revolutionary
War. Two great Poles who were heroes of this struggle
—Thaddeus Kosciuszko and Casimir Pulaski—are
known to every schoolchild studying the history of the
United States. Neither one was a citizen of the country
for which he fought, but both became bonded to
America by service in the cause of common liberty.
Their names have become as celebrated as those of
Thomas Jefferson and John Adams and other Ameri-
can champions of freedom.

About 1800, the total Polish population in the
United States stood at some five hundred. Already, the
character of immigration had changed, due to the
crushing political changes in Poland. The Polish political exile was finding his way to American shores. In
three partitions, in 1772, 1793, and 1795, Poland was
apportioned among its three occupiers, ceasing to be a
state but yet continuing as a people and civilization.
Russia absorbed the bulk of the land and inhabitants,
followed by Prussia and Austria. Poland's loss of state-
hood had many far-reaching effects, one of them being
to disperse Poles throughout the world. During the
early decades of the 1800's, the exodus was heightened

after various armed insurrections, with participants forced to flee in the face of imprisonment or death. As the result of one of these uprisings—the famous 1831 insurrection—some 7,000 refugees headed westward. A portion of the exiles remained in Europe to await further calls to arms in the cause of a free Poland, but others ventured across the Atlantic to take asylum and seek freedom in America.

Beginnings were hard for the intellectually-oriented political exiles who lost all possessions and position, espoused no trade, felt homesick, and were educated beyond any level of hard labor. Being individualistic, they went their own ways, scattering in every direction, trekking west into new territories. A few even reached California during the Gold Rush days. There were recommendations that a "Little Poland" be created in the United States by resettling a group of immigrants on land to be donated by Congress.

In 1834, the opportunity to establish such a colony seemed to appear with the arrival of some 235 Polish exiles who had participated in the 1831 uprising that broke out in Russian-dominated Poland. This assembly of wayfarers submitted a plea to Congress which, in part, said: "Although pilgrims in a foreign land, with nothing but the sad recollection of the past and hopes for the future, we wish to live a life of active industry, and become useful to the country of our adoption. . . ."

Commonwealth of POLAND in 1657

ACQUIRED BY . . .
RUSSIA
PRUSSIA
AUSTRIA

First Partition . . . 1772

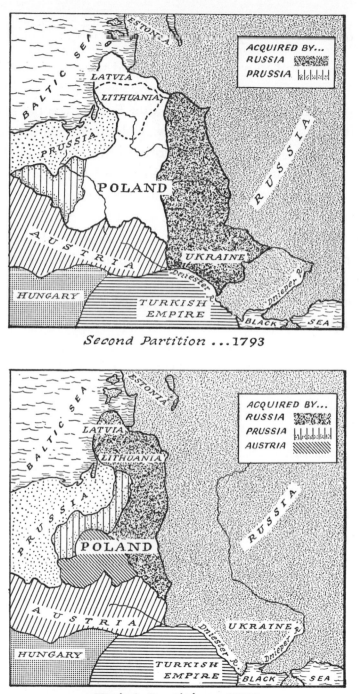

Second Partition ... 1793

Third Partition ... 1795

Their unhappy circumstances and those of their fellow countrymen prompted strong emotional sympathy in the United States. Poland, after France, was the first foreign country to win any widespread affinity in youthful America. Appeals to help the exiles and the cause of an independent Poland came from prominent Americans, among them the author, James Fenimore Cooper. He described Poland as "an heroic nation that should excite our esteem." Yet, somehow, the land grant for a "Little Poland" failed to materialize during the Jacksonian age, becoming lost in political and legal entanglements, although an original pledge was made through Congress.

But, twenty years later, a larger group of Poles arrived voluntarily to set down not a "Little Poland" but an American grass-roots settlement. Farm families, one hundred of them, left their familiar villages in the area of Silesia where they lived under Prussian domination for an odyssey of incredible hardship and adventure. Led by a Franciscan priest, Father Leopold Moczygemba, they set out for Texas, spurred by reports of its unfettered, expansive acres. After a journey of nine weeks, the immigrants arrived at Galveston. From there, they walked more than a hundred miles inland across wild prairies, the likes of which they had never seen. "We all had to be armed with sticks, hoes, or forks to fight off the snakes. . . . We lived in pits covered with brush wood," one of the settlers recounted in a letter home.

On Christmas eve, 1854, the group halted its march across Texas and gathered for the celebration of a Mass under a big oak tree. They called the spot Panna Maria in honor of the Virgin Mary, its designation to this day, and established here America's oldest Polish settlement. With them, they carried their ploughs and other farm implements, their bedding, their kitchen utensils and even a large cross from their old parish church. Other Poles from Silesia joined them in following years. Today, the church of these intrepid settlers and the general store at Panna Maria rank as Texas historical landmarks.

As soldiers, immigrant Poles brought to the battlefields of the Civil War, the extensive military experience they had gained in their own insurrections. During this war (when about thirty thousand Poles lived in the United States), at least five thousand saw battle, mostly on the side of the North. Brigadier-General Wladimir Krzyzanowski (happily nicknamed "Kriz" for short) fought at Gettysburg, Cross Keys, and Bull Run, winning many laurels and a later high customs office appointment. Two other brigadier-generals in the Union Army were Joseph Karge and Albin Schoepf; Karge, a scholar by disposition, distinguished himself as a cavalry leader and Schoepf led action in

Kentucky and Tennessee. The first officially recorded victim of the war happened to be the eighteen-year-old son of a Polish exile.

The real surge of Polish immigration began after the Civil War and the tide swelled in the 1880's with the bulk immigration of the peasants, who were to become laborers in America. These settlers came *za chlebem* (for bread). They were captivated partly by accounts of the immense wealth of the United States and absorbed fanciful tales—one, for example, which reported a treasure of pennies growing at the feet of the Statue of Liberty. Agents for steamship companies, a force not to be discounted in the stimulation of migration, avidly recruited passengers in the eastern and southern lands of Europe. The immigrants bought passage with funds they had saved, begged, or borrowed.

By the advent of World War I, the number of Poles in the United States had grown by millions. During immigration, however, many of the newcomers "lost" their nationality. Because Poland did not exist as an independent state, officials tended to register the immigrants as Prussian, Russian, or Austrian, depending on the section of partitioned Poland from which they came. This made it impossible to determine with any real accuracy, the total number of Poles who settled in the United States. To this day, no exact figure can be quoted for Poles and those of Polish descent living in America. Estimates from qualified sources range from six to ten million, with the higher statistic preferred by popular mass publications. Probably, six million represents a reasonable total.

How very little the mass of Polish immigrants brought with them! They had skills of the soil but only a few grades of formal education, no knowledge of English, only the material possessions they could carry and pocket money of a few dollars. Yet, their less visible "baggage" was impressive: A love and thirst for freedom, a sense of loyalty and honor, religious fervor, vast physical and ethnical strength, and a dedication to work. Their rush to get work led at least two-thirds of all the newcomers to large manufacturing and mining areas. They took backbreaking jobs with backbreaking risks; they went into coal mines, steel mills, foundries, machine shops, quarries, and factories. States like New York, Pennsylvania, Illinois, Michigan, New Jersey, Wisconsin, Ohio, Massachusetts, and Connecticut experienced an influx of Poles. Chicago eventually counted more Poles than lived in Warsaw, and other localities among them Buffalo, Detroit, New York, Philadelphia, Milwaukee, Cleveland, Newark, Toledo, Pittsburgh, Baltimore, Boston, Jersey City, and New Britain, Connecticut—had strong Polish segments.

Wisconsin, where pioneer Poles settled in Portage

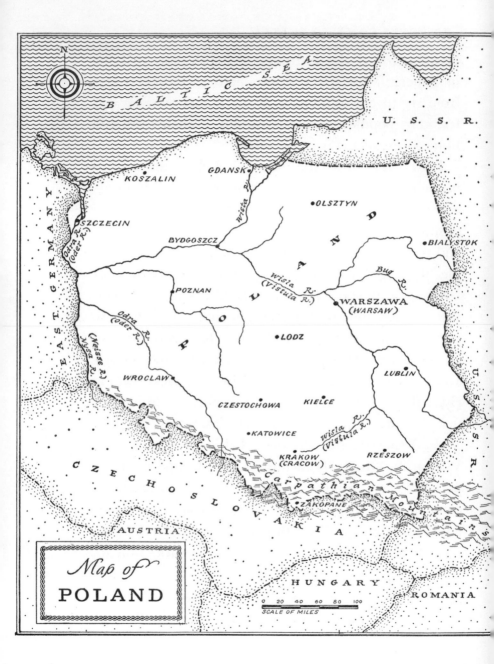

Map of
POLAND

SCALE OF MILES
0 20 40 60 80 100

county as early as 1855, listed the largest number of Polish settlements. Places like Pulaski, Krakow, Sobieski, and Lublin dotted the face of the state. The story is told about a visitor arriving at a characteristic Polish-American city called Stevens Point and inquiring what the population was of this Wisconsin city. The answer, from a hotel clerk, was immediate. "Polish," he said.

Different areas attracted Poles for different reasons. New England, especially the Connecticut valley, lured settlers who could not bear to leave the tilling of soil to others. The Middle Atlantic states offered employment in the coal, steel, and textile industries. The central states, especially those around the Great Lakes, welcomed Poles to the automotive and other heavy industries. By dint of their numbers, Polish workers became a factor in the permanent establishment of labor unions in the United States. Some of the immigrants went west into lumber camps and reached California, too. In some areas, cities and whole neighborhoods took on a definite Polish flavor, in language and tone.

At no place has the impact of the Polish immigrant been more closely studied than at Hamtramck, a community within the confines of Detroit where Poles came to constitute 70 per cent of the population. Sociologist Arthur Evans Wood, in a study published in 1955, tagged Hamtramck "a fascinating cultural island." He described it as "highly self-conscious, proud of its Polish tradition, resentful of criticism and confident of its economic advantages." His dissection of the development of the community, however, is not completely flattering, though he does suggest that Poles have been exemplary Americans. And it was a president of one of the great automotive works at Detroit who firmly proclaimed: "Hamtramck is made up of solid, hard-working citizens—the kind of folks who are the core of a great industrial nation."

Just how did the Polish immigrant fit into his new setting? His first concern, after finding a job and a place to live, was to attend to religious, social, and cultural needs. More than any other single influence, Roman Catholicism nourished and united Poles in America. Poland, it must be remembered, was converted as a nation to Christianity more than a thousand years ago, and the church became a force in keeping alive the national aspirations of the land. In the United States, the parish church and school became a center for the preservation of language and culture, as well as for social assembly. The parish priest represented a pivot around which immigrant Poles congregated.

Different members of the clergy early gained some fame—Father Waclaw Kruszka, for example, was an early historian of Poles in America; Father Francis

Dzierozynski helped to launch several Jesuit institutions of higher learning in the United States; and the Reverend Francis Hodur organized the Polish National Catholic church in America, which is not a part of Roman Catholicism. Poles contributed immensely to the development of the Catholic church in America. Some experts say that at least one out of every six Catholics in America is of Polish background.

Around "Polonia"—a term identifying Poles and their descendants—a whole network of societies, clubs, and institutions sprang up, along with a Polish language press. Goals of patriotism, fraternity, and service were espoused by organizations like the Polish National Alliance, the Polish Roman Catholic Union, and the Polish Falcons. Women had their societies with social, cultural, and charitable aims; special interest units, like veterans, formed their own groups. Educational organizations even came to include Alliance College at Cambridge Springs, Pennsylvania. Associations of wider intellectual and cultural impact came somewhat later, with the Kosciuszko Foundation, begun in 1925 in New York, and the Polish Institute of Arts and Sciences (1942), also headquartered in New York. In Chicago, in 1926, a first Polish Arts club was founded and similar endeavors scattered in a wide selection of cities now exist under the umbrella of the American Council of Polish Cultural Clubs. Significantly, these groups persistently promote at the community level an appreciation of Polish accomplishments in many fields —art, literature, music, crafts, folklore—and have interested the non-Polish neighbor in the culture of Poland.

As was the case with other nationalities transplanted to America, Poles had to meet, talk, worship, fraternize, and bolster up one another to convince themselves they still had an identity before they could feel either settled or secure in their changed surroundings. An immediate longing was for American citizenship, for this achievement truly proved they belonged to their new world.

The road to this prize was paved by tortuous learning, especially as requirements of knowledge became more stringent. Immigrants enrolled in evening classes for citizenship or else were tutored at home by their own sons or daughters as these children gained advantage from public or parochial school education. First-generation youngsters were special mentors of naturalization, for the road to citizenship was a long one for the many immigrants scarcely literate. Peasants in Poland had no real opportunity for formal schooling, particularly in those lands held by the Russians and Prussians. This was not the age of compulsory schooling, and what did the occupying powers of Poland care about teaching serfs anything? Many first-generation youngsters remembered the repeated admonition of their parents: What you have in your head, no one can take away. Immigrants looked upon extended education as a remarkable gift, one they joyfully bequeathed their children by settling in the United States.

What stubborn words had to be coaxed from the faltering tongues of a mother or father by their American-born children to help them win naturalization papers! They were repeated around the kitchen table or on the porch steps on a summer's day—words like con-sti-tu-tion-al, leg-is-la-tive, ju-di-cia-ry. In exasperation, the would-be learners sometimes took refuge in their own facile language, exploding with: *"Do licha, co to jest!"* ("What the devil is that!") When the wondrous time came to take the oath of citizenship, they did it with tears of disbelief and pride. Sometimes, they became so overwhelmed by the sentiment and emotion they attached to American citizenship they scarcely could raise their work-worn hands in pledge of their allegiance as they spoke it a first time.

How was the immigrant Pole of mass migration received and regarded in America? Variously. Most of the Poles arrived in America during the course of three and a half decades, flooding into cities and forming colonies of their own, colonies where they could do everything from buying bread to exchanging political views, all in their own tongue. Older-stock Americans were sure that the country was being "diluted" by these Slavs. Nationally, the mood turned mean when Congress enacted a quota system of restricted immigration directed against countries of eastern and southern Europe. Only in 1965 was a new Immigration Bill passed to undo some of the wrongs of this restrictive legislation.

The Poles, along with other newcomer nationalities, encountered intolerance. Some established American residents were condescending, others hostile. At times, Poles were dismissed simply as "greenhorns" and the term "Polak" (the proper designation in Polish for the nationality) became "Polack" and used in a derogatory sense. The Polish immigrant became a bunt for jokes contrived to point up a kind of stupor; this particular variety of humor survives to this day but appears to be passing into folklore. Different outside observers characterized the Poles as quarrelsome, factional, and beset by inferiority complexes. The children of immigrants sometimes were ridiculed, ostracized, or insulted with slang names by their contemporaries, and they tended to grow up with a negative sense of nationality. Within families, as well as from without, relationships knotted and warped.

Reared in an occupied Poland, immigrants had gaps in the knowledge of their own history, geography, and literature. Yet, artlessly, they managed to transmit the spirit, joy, and tradition of their background in easy, spontaneous ways that centered on holiday observances. Special foods, customs, dances, songs, and folklore caught some notice from non-Polish America—for example, the meatless series of dishes at *wigilia* or Christmas eve dinner; the Easter custom of decorating eggs called *pisanki;* the robust dances of the Polish mountaineers; the protracted merrymaking at weddings. *Pierogi* (filled dumplings), *barczsz* (beet soup), *kielbasa* (sausage), and a variety of pastries and cakes widely could be identified as Polish. Rightly or wrongly, the "polka" tended to become synonymous with Poles, even though the dance was Bohemian in origin. And "polonaise" was recognized as a dance, a Chopin composition, or a way to fix vegetables by turning them out with breadcrumbs fried golden in butter.

Certain traits came to be attributed to Poles—an infectious gaiety, a strong sense of individualism, a certain recklessness, rock-bound devotion to church, land, and country, and a rooted sentiment for culture and custom. They brought a definite mood and flavor to the communities where they lived, even a characteristic speech whereby they rather delightfully but not too grammatically mixed their native tongue and adopted language. Whole cities reflected the Polish influence in names like Poland, New York; Warsaw, Kentucky; and Pulaski, Virginia. The Poles came to have heroes shared not just with the United States but with the entire world. Who was unaware of the music of Frederic Chopin or the literary achievements of Joseph Conrad or the scientific feats of Marie Sklodowska-Curie? Schoolchildren could cite Nicholas Copernicus as the founder of modern astronomy.

Different factors helped to break down unreasonable attitudes toward Poles in the United States and to popularize them and their causes. Especially important was the resurrection of their native land after World War I. American Poles tended to take a sentimental attitude rather than a practical political approach to the problem of a reunited Poland. When, finally, thanks to the firm insistence of President Woodrow Wilson, a Polish republic emerged, Polish-Americans pointed to it with new pride and self-assurance. New Polish heroes appeared on the American scene and a last wave of immigrants came to the United States during and after World War II when Poland was subject to yet another partition and occupation, this time by Nazi Germany and the Soviet Union. These recent newcomers consisted of ex-soldiers, political exiles and professional people who could not or chose not to return to Poland under an emerging Polish Communist government. They injected a new element into Polish-American life, helping to emphasize that, in qualities of mind, Poles can be both diverse and profound.

He Died for American Freedom

Casimir Pulaski

> "I could not submit to stoop before the sovereigns of
> Europe, so I came here to hazard all for the freedom
> of America."

DASHING, gallant, reckless, handsome, of courtly
manner and noble birth, with a passionate commit-
ment to freedom, Casimir Pulaski was a storybook
hero. Had he not been part of history, one would be
tempted to call him a fairy tale prince. As it was, he
happened to be a count. When he arrived on American
shores in the dark year of 1777 to share the perils of the
Revolutionary War, he came to a country of which he
had little knowledge but to a cause—the struggle for
liberty—to which he was deeply pledged. His stay and
his service to the American colonies was brief—less
than two years—but his fame has endured the centuries
and his name is more familiar to Americans than that
of any other Polish hero. Many memorials in the

United States give permanent testimony to his contribution to the making of America.

The story of his life begins on a large and pleasant estate in the Masovia, a region of gentle, quiet landscape in the central plains of Poland. As the son of a country squire, young Casimir enjoyed a privileged childhood. His father, Count Joseph Pulaski, was a wealthy and successful jurist and was held in wide esteem. The family lived in a manor house at Winiary, near Warka, which can be seen today on a short excursion from Warsaw. Casimir's birth on March 4, 1747, was a happy event and his baptism in the family chapel on the estate represented an occasion for feasting and merrymaking for relatives and friends who came from far and wide. Historians tend to differ on some details of the young aristocrat's early life but they concur that he was raised as befitting a patriot and gentleman and groomed to be a "republican" in the lofty, Polish sense of the word, with devotion to duty and service to high causes ingrained in him.

While still a child, the future cavalry specialist learned to ride, with the coachmen on the estate supervising his progress. In joyous jaunts on horseback, the boy sped over the many acres of rolling land around him. His earliest schooling was at a nearby parish school. At home, Casimir learned much about the social and political stirrings of the times by listening to the animated discussions when friends and associates of his father gathered and wine flowed from big casks stored in the cellar. In his teens, the boy was sent to Warsaw to study, again under Catholic guidance. At fifteen, he joined the guard of Duke Charles of Courtland in what today is Latvia. He served this patron in a kind of apprenticeship, learning skills of defense and combat.

So far as is known, Pulaski never had any formal military training; he learned from practice, books, and experience. The real experience began upon his return to Poland, when he considered himself ready for military duties in protection and help for his native land as neighboring powers threatened, with Russia, Prussia, and Austria moving toward aquisition of land and people.

Casimir's father had founded an organization called the Confederation of the Bar; essentially, this was a Catholic resistance movement which united a segment of the gentry in opposition to any foreign encroachment of Poland. The movement took its name from the village of Bar in the Podolia province and it was organized as the specter of partition began to loom. At this time in Poland's complicated history, the reigning king—destined to be the last king of the country—was Stanislaus II who was, to all effect, a puppet of the Russians, and the so-called "favorite" of Catherine the

Great of Russia. He failed to raise any resistance to power-hungry aggression on the part of Russia.

On January 29, 1768, the Confederation of the Bar proclaimed an insurrection against foreign troops on Polish soil. Casimir, then twenty-one years old, joined in the active rebellion. He soon proved himself a determined and skillful soldier, meeting and defeating the enemy in various skirmishes undertaken by the insurrectionists.

An incident vividly indicative of Pulaski's incredible will to win and his tenaciousness in battle is recorded in Polish annals. Once, when Pulaski was besieged at the headquarters of a religious community toward the south of Poland, he discovered—after repelling the Cossacks in their initial assaults—that his garrison had run short of ammunition to continue the battle. Undaunted, he ordered everything which possibly could be used as a weapon to be thrown into the fight; then, even nails and broken glass showered the startled enemy.

In 1770, Pulaski and the revolutionists occupied the famous pilgrimage center at Czestochowa, a fortress-like monastery and other buildings surrounded by stone walls, and made it a base for future operations. With daring sallies, the insurrectionists conducted a relentless guerrilla warfare against the Cossacks.

When, in 1772, the shocking news came that Austria
had joined with Prussia and Russia to partition Poland
and that the king had acceded to this program, the
gallant fighters had no choice but to flee. Young
Pulaski was sentenced to death by a high criminal
court which accused him of instigating an unsuccessful
plot to kidnap the king. During his lifetime, Pulaski
protested that he had not been a party to this plot but
protestations did not dissolve the sentence hanging
over him. While, in Polish history, unpopular kings
existed, there also existed what amounted to a code of
honor that no violence be attempted against the person
of the king. The charge against Pulaski, therefore, was
a most serious accusation.

Traveling disguised, Pulaski left the country during
the course of 1772, never to return again. Members of
his family, too, were forced into exile and their estate
and wealth taken from them.

His banishment led him to Turkey where he tried to
interest the Turks in marching against the Russians,
but to no avail. Eventually, Pulaski reached Paris, late
in 1775. Again, he made efforts to get help for hapless
Poland. About this time, the funds he had been able to
take with him from his native land gave out. Penniless, and close to starving, he was cast into a debtors'
prison in Marseilles and lived with the lowest of crimi-
nals. He was released and aided when his plight came

to the attention of friends and officials in the French government.

In 1776, Pulaski heard the electrifying news that a war of independence had broken out on the American continent. He decided his destiny was in America, fighting to aid the colonists. Because of his experience in Poland where he had commanded up to 18,000 men, he could count himself among those seasoned in the art of battle.

Friends interceded for Pulaski with Benjamin Franklin, representative of the colonists in Paris, who engaged the Pole for service in the Revolutionary War. The exiled Pulaski probably most precisely expressed his strong motivation in seeking service in America when he wrote to a well-known French historian and confidant: "I would rather live free, or die for liberty. I suffer more because I cannot avenge myself against the tyranny of those who seek to oppress humanity. That is why I want to go to America. . . ."

Franklin recommended Pulaski to George Washington as "famous throughout Europe for his bravery and conduct in defense of the liberties of this country. . . ."

The volunteer soldier set sail for a land he was fated never to leave. Upon landing in Massachusetts (historians quibble about just where he landed but Boston seems the most likely port), he reported to Commander-in-Chief Washington at headquarters in Penn-

sylvania. He received a letter that asked the Continental Congress to grant him a commission.

Not willing to remain idle until Congress had acted
on this request, Pulaski joined the army as a volunteer
and went into battle at Brandywine on September 11,
1777. Here he scouted the enemy by riding close to the
British lines at great personal danger. Through his
reconnaissance, the advance of the redcoats was detected in such numbers as to threaten Washington
himself and part of the top command. Some accounts
credit Pulaski with saving the main American army
from total destruction at a battle which the British
won. Congress thought highly enough of his daring
and bravery to award him a commission as brigadier-
general in charge of the American cavalry forces.
Pulaski came to be regarded as the best and most
expert horseman in the American service.

History was to confer upon the fighting equestrian
the title of "Father of the American Cavalry," but
the path to accomplishment of this goal was beset
with disappointments, frustrations, and obstacles. Soon
enough, Pulaski discovered the cavalry was a neglected
branch of the military forces and that it was not a concept of American strategy to groom this division for
independent operations. He found he had neither the
men nor the arms to launch any military actions of
much import. Supposedly, four regiments of more

than seven hundred men came under his command, but Pulaski found almost all the cavalry divided for special services and duties.

He went into battle, however, with whatever forces were available and continued to distinguish himself. At Germantown, Pulaski helped to cover the retreat of American divisions. At Haddonfield, near Camden, New Jersey, he aided in the defeat of the British and had his own horse shot from under him.

Fired with an ambition to mold a crack fighting unit, Pulaski reorganized, trained, and drilled the American cavalry. He supplied this branch of the army with its first set of service regulations and tried to inspire his men with discipline and spirit. He even formed a detachment armed with Polish lances. But, constantly, there was a shortage of supplies, money, and equipment. Pulaski wrote imploring letters to Congress and Washington seeking the necessary means to perfect the cavalry. His entreaties, however, failed to get results.

There were other problems, too. Some officers, particularly those of higher rank, chafed at taking orders from a foreigner, however eminent. "The Count" ran into barriers and unsettling situations because he had no full knowledge of the English language and American habits. Eventually, he concluded that too many frictions were developing and that a lack of harmony existed among certain officers, partly on his account. So, he resigned his commission in March, 1778, and presented to Washington a plan for raising an independent corps. He suggested the corps consist of sixty-eight cavalrymen armed with lances and two hundred infantrymen.

Washington recommended the plan to Congress which did vote the formation of what was to become the celebrated Pulaski Legion. It evolved into one of the few detachments predominantly foreign in its make-up, with members mostly German-Americans, and officers primarily French, German, and Polish.

Pulaski bore various costs in establishing the Legion with funds he raised himself from Europe, and estimates of his own outlay run into thousands of dollars. He did this gladly because he was so anxious to establish the corps and because the constant demands of Congress for exact accountings of money it provided rather exasperated him.

During the recruitment of members, Pulaski visited Bethlehem, Pennsylvania, where he ordered a special banner for his Legion from the Moravian nuns. The crimson satin banner bore an all-seeing eye of God, thirteen stars, and a Latin motto meaning "Union makes for valor." The great American poet, Henry Wadsworth Longfellow, immortalized this banner in a touching poem called "Hymn of the Moravian Nuns of

Bethlehem" that bespoke the future and fate of Pulaski:

> Take thy banner! May it wave
> Proudly o'er the good and brave;
> When the battle's distant wail
> Breaks the sabbath of our vale,
> When the clarion's music thrills
> To the hearts of those lone hills,
> When the spear in conflict shakes,
> And the strong lance shivering breaks. . . .
>
> Take thy banner! and if e'er
> Thou shouldst press the soldier's bier,
> And the muffled drum should beat
> To the tread of mournful feet,
> Then this crimson flag shall be
> Martial cloak and shroud for thee.

In September, 1778, the Legion, so colorful in appearance and banner, prepared to go into battle. The Legionnaires were ordered to New Jersey where they fought at Egg Harbor, forcing the British to withdraw. Pulaski spent the winter of 1778-1779 in the northwestern part of New Jersey and complained about the lack of battle activity. In February, Congress resolved that the Legion should move south to the area of vigorous fighting. Pulaski strengthened the corps with new recruits and set out on his way in the spring.

The Legionnaires reached Charleston, South Carolina, at the very time the British were demanding that the city surrender to them. Pulaski led his unit in an attack on the advancing column of British, pushing the Tories back in disorder, but at a considerable loss of his own corpsmen. Importantly, the siege of Charleston was lifted and the British retreated farther south.

When, in September, a strategic plan was worked out for the recapture of Savannah, Georgia, from the British, Pulaski and his Legion were part of the plan. The Legionnaires attacked British outposts along their route to Savannah, as ordered, and then successfully joined French troops for an all-out drive.

The British were called upon to surrender but without avail and American troops launched an ill-fated assault on the city, not realizing fully the extent of the entrenched British forces. In the plan of attack, three columns of French soldiers were to strike at certain sections of the British line. Pulaski was to follow the leader of one of these columns to the main attack with his cavalry.

The fighting was fierce and the French leader Pulaski was to assist fell wounded. Heedlessly, Pulaski rushed to the fore and into the breach to rally the column and the charge. But he, too, fell, wounded in the thigh by grapeshot, a cluster of small iron balls used as a cannon charge.

Eyewitness accounts vary as to the exact details of Pulaski's last stand, but those who saw him fall gave testimony to his exemplary conduct and great bravery. One of the officers of the Legion later described it: "We sped like Knights into the peril. . . . Imploring the help of the Almighty, Pulaski shouted 'Forward' and we rode at full speed after him, the earth resounding under the hoofs of our chargers. . . ."

The attack ended in failure and two days later the end came for Pulaski. He died, in great pain, on board the ship, *Wasp,* in Savannah harbor. The most skilled surgeons could not save his life. While probably not mortal in itself, the wound became infected and gangrenous. Pulaski's body was buried at sea. A hero of two continents closed his fight for freedom at the age of thirty-two.

Different depictions of Pulaski characterize him as being small in stature but vital and strong, with high Slavic cheekbones, a trim mustache, and a compelling, clear-eyed glance. In personal qualities, he was described as sincere, candid, generous. In those who served under him, he was able to inspire courage, loyalty, and zeal. His fierce espousal of principle always was evident. Doubtless, Pulaski himself best expressed his absolute dedication to the ideal of liberty when he wrote to Congress: ". . . I could not submit to stoop before the sovereigns of Europe, so I came to hazard all for the freedom of America."

Some historians tend to discredit Pulaski's accomplishments as exaggerated and to discount his bravery as foolhardy. But the fact remains that here was a foreigner who proved himself a relentless warrior in the cause of American independence. No matter that he may have espoused a mad heroism in the proud tradition of his own people and the land of his birth; it surely was heroism hard to match. He carried very early to the New World the later motto that would be identified with Poles fighting freedom's battle in different corners of the globe: "For our liberty and yours."

Cities, towns, monuments, parks, and even bridges have been named in honor of Casimir Pulaski in the United States. At Savannah, a monument was built to him in 1853—the cornerstone of which had been laid earlier—and a fort erected for the defense of Savannah also bore his name. Monuments can be found in many other places, among them Milwaukee, Wisconsin; Washington, D.C.; and Baltimore, Maryland. On the map, cities bearing the name of Pulaski are located in various states, including Tennessee, Virginia, Pennsylvania, New York, Illinois, Kentucky, and Wisconsin. Almost every state in the Union has a commemorative tribute to the gallant general, whether in the name of a street, town, park, square, school, or highway.

A Pulaski stamp was issued by the United States government on the occasion of the 150th anniversary of his death. Nationally, the day of Pulaski's death— October 11—has been proclaimed a Memorial Day. The late President John F. Kennedy issued annual proclamations on this occasion and was the speaker at the Pulaski Day parade and program in Buffalo, New York, in 1962. At that event, President Kennedy said of the noble Polish-American hero: "General Pulaski was not an American. He had been on these shores less than two years before he died. He represented a different culture, a different language, a different way of life. But he had the same love of liberty as the people of this country, and therefore, he was an American as much as he was a Pole."

He Left an American Legacy

Thaddeus Kosciuszko

> "He was idolized by the soldiers for his bravery and
> beloved and respected by the officers for the goodness
> of his heart, and the great qualities of his mind. His
> fame will last as long as liberty remains upon the earth
> . . . ."

MANY LAURELS GRACE the name of Thaddeus Kosciuszko, a hero to the entire civilized world. He has
been applauded as the purest son of liberty, the last of
the knights, the first among gallant patriots, the most
unpretentious of leaders. Respected and loved as a
human being, Kosciuszko embodied, for many, the
best of the aspirations which purport to define Poles.
The famous general, a hero in America and Europe,
was brave without being proud; talented without
being arrogant; dedicated without being overbearing;
and sentimental without being maudlin. His sense of
justice recognized no limitations—it extended to na-

tions, races, and individuals; he was not a champion of rights for an isolated age but for all ages. Of him, George Washington said: "No one has a higher respect and veneration for your character than I have."

Kosciuszko left a remarkable legacy in the America of Revolutionary days. As a fortifications engineer, he spent more than two years building the sturdy bastion of West Point, the achievement inseparably linked with his name. As a military strategist, he selected battle sites and constructed entrenchments which contributed significantly to American victories during he Revolution. As a volunteer soldier, he fought in the ranks of the Yankee army and went down in history as the "Father of the American Artillery." As a defender of human rights, he early saw the injustice of the position of the Negro and willed that the modest fortune he accumulated in the United States be used to buy freedom and training for slaves.

This record in itself would be enough to insure its holder a place in posterity but, for Kosciuszko, there must be added even more illustrious achievement in his native Poland where he led Polish forces in the final struggle before the last partition of the country. While he was the earliest foreign patriot to heed the call of the "shot heard round the world" at Lexington, he triggered similar repercussions in the world with his rash and last fight for Poland's freedom.

His life began in an eastern province of Poland in a small place with the long name of Mereczowszczyzna on February 12, 1746. His father was a member of the middle gentry, of old Polish stock. Young Thaddeus obtained his early schooling at home, as this was the custom for his social class. Later, he attended a private school operated by a religious order where the subjects included languages, philosophy, history, and mathematics. When Thaddeus was twelve years old, his father died; the mother was left the care of four children.

By his own inclination, Thaddeus became enamored of heroes of antiquity, admiring them for their idealism, single-mindedness, and romanticism. His spare-time reading concentrated on the classics and other serious works. In 1765, after deciding he wanted to be a soldier, he succeeded in being admitted to the Royal Military School in Warsaw. This school offered a curriculum of liberal general studies along with the opportunity to train in military science. Kosciuszko was graduated four years later with the rank of captain and a fine scholastic record. As a promising cadet, he attracted the notice of Prince Adam Czartoryski—a member of one of the wealthiest landowning families of the country—and received a year's scholarship to continue his military engineering studies in France.

Upon his return to Poland, the ambitious student

found little opportunity for his talents and encountered conditions generally depressing. He had financial problems, because his share in the family estate was small and, in time, had problems in love, as well. Kosciuszko fell in love, apparently irretrievably so, with the daughter of a high political official. It was an unlucky courtship, for the father had set his mind on a marriage of wealth and position for his attractive, dark-haired daughter. The mutual love between the two young people led them to an elopement which was intercepted by a searching party sent out by the father. Accounts relate that there was a skirmish in which Kosciuszko fought and was wounded. The father forbade his daughter ever to see Kosciuszko again and warned the star-crossed soldier never to set foot in his house. Later, the daughter, Ludwika Sosnowska, married a wealthy rival from one of Poland's first families. Kosciuszko never married.

The dejected suitor left Poland and returned to Paris where reports of the American Revolution stirred his imagination and soldier's interest. He borrowed money to make the trip to America, arriving in Philadelphia during the summer of 1776. Kosciuszko came at an opportune time. The Declaration of Independence had been proclaimed only a few weeks before and while recruits in the cause of liberty for the colonies were numerous and resolute, they also were ignorant and undisciplined in the arts of war. The Pennsylvania Committee of Defense hired Kosciuszko as a military engineer to draw up plans to fortify the Delaware River. His successful execution of this task gained him a commission as a colonel of engineers in the Continental Army.

In the spring of 1777, Kosciuszko joined the northern army under General Horatio Gates who came to esteem the young Pole's abilities and judgment. He advised the general to entrench his forces at Bemis Heights and to build a stronghold crowning these heights, in carrying out a plan to defend Saratoga. The Americans beat back the British and cut off their escape route during this decisive battle. In official reports, Kosciuszko—because of his strategic fortification —shared in this important victory at Saratoga.

The next spring, the volunteer engineer was sent to West Point to fortify the heights there. The Hudson River had primary importance in the Revolutionary War; Kosciuszko's assignment was to make West Point such a citadel as to dissuade the enemy from all temptation to try to take the lands. He worked at the task for two years, until August, 1780. The work continued almost without interruption, even though there were scant allowances of food and supplies for his engineers and aides during the terrible winter of 1779-1780. Almost a wilderness when he came to the spot, Kosciuszko left on the heights at West Point a well-contrived and pleasing bastion that future generations of cadets training in the highest military standards could appreciate.

There were many touching tales connected with Kosciuszko's assignment at West Point. The compassionate Pole, distressed by the misery of the English prisoners of war, divided with them his own modest rations and used his savings to buy them food. For his aesthetic pleasure and to nourish his poetic soul, the military engineer planted a flower garden in a secluded nook among the rocks, carrying earth to the barren spot in baskets. Here he spent leisure hours in quietude and contemplation. Who knows what he thought and dreamed about—perhaps the plight of his own country, his youth, his lost love. . . . To this very day, this unexpected corner of charm and brightness survives and bears the name of Kosciuszko Garden.

Not especially prepossessing in appearance, Kosciuszko was short, with direct, piercing eyes, a firm-set mouth, and rather a prominent nose. In day-to-day life, he was described as tireless, modest, considerate, with a wonderously simple and open character. He once wrote: "The principles of decency which have been impressed upon me since earliest childhood have had such a strong influence on my feelings, that any action made against my deep convictions makes me extremely malcontent."

While a dedicated fighter for freedom, he yet was a thoughtful soldier. One of his swords was inscribed with what seemed to exemplify his philosophy in the rush or heat of battle. On the blade was engraved: "Do not draw me out without necessity" and "Do not put me in without honor."

In August, 1780, Kosciuszko, at his own request, was transferred to the southern area of army operations after the main fighting shifted to this region. He served under General Nathanael Greene who spoke of him with the warmest praise. The two became close friends, as a collection of letters attest. Kosciuszko made the entire campaign in the south under Greene until the evacuation of Charleston. When not fighting in the ranks, he made surveys of fields of operation and planned and executed ways of rapidly transporting troops, a matter of importance in campaigns launched in a terrain of rivers and swamps. The Pole also displayed vast skill in the use of artillery and often was more conspicuous as a leader of the artillery than an engineer.

Kosciuszko returned north in the springtime of 1783, after American independence was assured. Congress tardily made him a brigadier-general for "long, faithful and meritorious services." He, too, was elected to the exclusive Society of the Cincinnati, an organization limited to officers of the Continental Army—a rare honor for a foreigner. Before he returned to

Poland, Congress rewarded him by entitling him to a grant of public land and making provision to pay more than $12,000 in salary. Contrary to common belief, Kosciuszko never was accorded American citizenship, although his service of seven years in the Revolution rather seemed to naturalize him by deed if not in fact as an American.

There is little question that he felt very close to America and its people. In 1779, he wrote in a letter to General Gates: "I suppose myself to be at this time more than half a Yankee." While he was in America, he became very deeply involved in his new surroundings, experiences, and friends; only meager accounts of his doings and whereabouts reached Poland, for he had little time to write. Preparing to leave the United States in 1783, Kosciuszko requested of General Greene: "I beseech you to furnish the most detailed information on the state of public affairs. . . . Having lived in the country and with its inhabitants, just by being there, I feel as they do, a good patriot." Undeniably, Kosciuszko carried with him political and social concepts of the Revolution and the rising America that were to influence him and his actions in coming struggles for Polish freedom.

At the age of thirty-nine, in July of 1784, Kosciuszko bade America farewell but not good-by, as it turned out. Upon arriving in Poland, he discovered he had gained some fame from his American military service. But he kept himself aloof from public life, retreating into almost rural retirement for several years on his paternal estate at Siechnowicze. With growing change and turmoil within and without Poland, Kosciuszko, in time, did put his military talents to work in the interests of his homeland. He devised a militia system for Poland's army and, in the spring of 1792, led a small force in resistance against the Russians. Significant internal reforms were in the process of evolvement and culminated in the famous Constitution of May 3, 1791, which aimed at a widening of rights in Poland and bettering the condition of peasants. But the powerful neighbors of the Poles again stirred and in 1793 the second partition of the country—by Russia and Prussia—occurred. There was no opportunity to carry out reforms.

Kosciuszko was forced to flee, but only temporarily. He was called back, secretly, to lead the uprising of 1794 as the supreme commander of the Polish army in a brave but futile war of liberation. He began his campaign at Cracow, the ancient capital of Poland, and rallied what must have been the first poor people's army of Europe. Aware, from his American experience, that ragged, untutored citizen soldiers could win great victories when fired by a strong cause, he inspired the Polish peasants to arms. These volunteers came carrying scythes as weapons to fight under the banner of Kosciuszko. They met the Russians at a place called Raclawice and defeated them. One of the most celebrated portraits of Kosciuszko shows him in peasant's garb which he donned in tribute to his remarkable army.

His leadership influenced other segments of the Polish population—the townsmen, for example—to take up arms, and the growing forces of the insurrectionists brought significant gains. Warsaw was liberated and much of Poland's ancient territory had been recovered before Kosciuszko and his army of liberation was stopped at Maciejowice by a combined force of Russians and Prussians. The stubborn fighter was wounded and carried away into Russia as a prisoner of war. This was the end of the insurrection and, in 1795, a third partition erasing Poland from the map of Europe took place, between Russia, Prussia, and Austria. The heroic efforts toward freedom, however, and Kosciuszko's example deeply affected all Poles.

For two years, Kosciuszko was imprisoned in the dungeons of St. Petersburg and finally was liberated by Czar Paul I. Again in exile, the long-suffering soldier traveled to America by way of Finland, Sweden, and England. After a stormy Atlantic crossing of almost two months, Kosciuszko arrived at Philadelphia where citizens accorded him a triumphal welcome. The greeters unhitched the horses from the carriage bearing Kosciuszko and pulled it themselves to his lodging place.

He traveled and spent time with different prominent friends, including Thomas Jefferson, then Secretary of State. It was Jefferson who wrote of Kosciuszko: "He is as pure a son of liberty as I have ever known, and of that liberty which is to go to all, and not to the few and rich alone." Everywhere Kosciuszko went he was greeted with respect and honor; his gracious and learned conversation enlivened many a gathering. He traveled with his former aide-de-camp, Julian Ursyn Niemcewicz, a poet and chronicler who wrote widely about America and published the first original European biography of George Washington.

The welcomed guest planned to settle in America but fate decided otherwise. A secret summons took him back to Europe the next year, 1798, when Napoleon promised to restore Poland to her rank among nations. Before he left, Kosciuszko made out his last will and testament, a document quite unparalleled in foresight and generosity. Kosciuszko asked that the estate deeded him by Congress be used to buy liberty and training for Negro slaves in the United States. The testament, dated May 5, authorized Jefferson, as the executor, to ". . . employ the whole hereof in purchasing Negroes from among his own or any others, and giving them liberty in my name; in giving them an education in trade or otherwise in having them instructed, for their new conditions in the duties of morality, which may make them good neighbors, good fathers and mothers, husbands and wives, in their duty as citizens; teaching them to be defenders of their liberty and country, of the good order of society, and in whatsoever may make them happy and useful."

As a believer in social justice for all people, Kosciuszko recognized the plight of the Negroes, comparing it in some ways with the conditions suffered by the Polish peasants in a society where the landed nobility enjoyed extensive privileges. Not only did he see the unjust circumstances of the Negroes, but he saw, as clearly, the solution in liberty and education—a solution that could have prevented, by widespread application, future turmoil in the struggle of the American Negro for equal rights. He succinctly expressed his views on liberty when he declared: "Certain people believe that a nation must be enlightened before giving it liberty. As for me, I believe the contrary—that is to say, if one wishes to enlighten a people or nation, one must liberate them."

Upon his return to Europe, hopes and plans he nourished to liberate his homeland were dashed; he sadly discovered that Poland had become a pawn on the chessboard of European politics and that promises, although voiced, were void. Kosciuszko, from his Paris headquarters, tried to do what he possibly could. While in France, he rendered an additional service to America by writing, in 1800, a treatise called "Manoueuvres of Horse Artillery." Prepared in French, it was published in translation in New York and provided an effective system for organization of the American artillery. The United States fought the War of 1812 using these artillery instructions.

Kosciuszko, who was made an honorary citizen of France, eventually left the country to spend his last years in a quiet town in Switzerland at the home of the brother of a former Swiss ambassador to France. Residents of the town, called Soleure or Solothurn, in the Jura mountain region, came to know and respect their distinguished guest. They remembered his kind manner, his concern for the poor, and his excellent horsemanship. Many stories are told about how Kosciuszko visited the cottages of the poor with gifts of medicine, food, and money and, sometimes when he was out riding or walking, he stopped to help peasants working in the fields. He followed almost a monastic schedule, rising daily at five or six o'clock in the morning, and his self-imposed duties included tutoring the children of the family with which he lived. His Swiss chroniclers put him down as a man simple in manner and way of life and of profound religious conviction.

In April of 1817, Kosciuszko made out a will for disposition of his European holdings and in it gave freedom to the peasants living on land under his title in Poland. Partly, that testament read: "Deeply convinced that servitude is contrary to the law of nature and to the prosperity of the people, I declare in this document that it be forever abolished in my estate at Siechnowicze. . . . I, therefore, consider the inhabitants of the villages living on this estate as free citizens and owners without any restrictions of the lands which I possess. For their own welfare, and for the good of the country, I urge them to establish schools and to spread education."

That same year, on October 15, the hero died, away from both his beloved Poland and America. The scene of his death—the modest, sparsely furnished quarters where a votive representation of a familiar Polish Madonna hung over his canopied bed—has been preserved as a museum in Soleure. His remains were transferred from Switzerland to Poland in 1819 and installed in the crypt of Wawel at Cracow, the burial place of kings and great men of the country. But the people, the ordinary people whom he so inspired and for whom he fought so long, constructed their own monument to him, outside Cracow. They raised an immense mound of earth—carrying soil in wagons, pails, wheelbarrows, and even their bare hands—and this is known as the Mound of Kosciuszko.

Countless memorials and monuments honor Kosciuszko around the world. In the United States, Washington, West Point, Chicago, Milwaukee, Cleveland and Boston are among cities housing monuments. Many American place names commemorate him. A stamp honoring him was issued in the United States in 1933. The tributes lauding Kosciuszko would fill volumes. It was General William Harrison, the ninth president of the United States, who so portrayed him: "He was remarkable, throughout his service, for all the qualities which adorn the human character. His heroic valor in the field could only be equalled by his moderation and affability in the walks of private life. He was idolized by soldiers for his bravery, and beloved and respected by the officers for the goodness of his heart, and the great qualities of his mind. His fame will last as long as liberty remains upon the earth. . . ."

While some heroes are worshiped, Kosciuszko represents the illustrious warrior who endures as truly beloved. Those who served with or under this hero caught inspiration not so much from his genius but, more importantly, from the flame of his idealism, the fire of his zeal, the warmth of his vast humanity.

Pioneer, Explorer, and Trader

Anthony Sadowski

"He penetrated very early into Ohio as an Indian trader . . . and by the end of the eighteenth century, Sadowski and his descendants covered a large part of the middle west with pioneer traces."

AMONG THE EARLIEST immigrants from Poland who gained recognition in colonial records of America was a frontiersman called Anthony Sadowski. No complete historical annals exist by which to trace the step-by-step wilderness career of this hardy settler, but the biographical information available in official documents and family records advances him as an early Daniel Boone. Trail blazer, explorer, trader in furs, and negotiator with the Indians, Sadowski set a fearless pattern of pioneering continued by other family members who helped to win western stretches in Virginia, Kentucky, and Tennessee for the United States. Theodore Roosevelt, in his epic work, *The Winning of the*

West, salutes the Sadowskis as "a most respectable family."

From land where he homesteaded in Pennsylvania in 1712, Anthony Sadowski ventured over the Alleghenies into Ohio on the heels of redskins crossing the mountains in increasing numbers and set up a trading post said to be the forerunner of the industrial community of Sandusky. There is a widespread belief that the place name, Sandusky, not just in Ohio but also nearby states, derives from Sadowski. Some historical evidence supports this belief but the weight of reference and research materials appears to credit the name of Sandusky to the Wyandot Indian phrase meaning "cool, clear water." Whatever the origin of the geographic designation, there is no question that the Pole, Sadowski, penetrated as a pioneer into Ohio and into the area where a city, county, river, and bay came to bear the name, Sandusky.

Colonial records set down the name, Sadowski, in many ways. Sadoski, Zadosky, Sowdowsky, Sadusky, and Sandusky represented some of the variations. In Polish, the beginning syllable of the name means "orchard." Properly pronounced in the original language, the name would seem, to the English-attuned ear, to be spelled differently from what it is. That the name could be changed by the American accent, carelessness in spelling, and a tendency to simplify hard-to-pro-

nounce syllables is not so surprising. Future generations of the family became Sandusky, through a grad-
ual evolution of the name.

Anthony, the family founder in America, probably
was born in the west central part of Poland and
stemmed from minor nobility. The year of his birth has
been pinpointed to about 1670. Not much is known
about his early training or education but judging from
his accomplishments in colonial America, he must have
had a thorough and classical schooling, with special
emphasis on languages. A great-granddaughter remembered him as speaking seven languages. In Pennsylvania, Sadowski was called upon to serve the provincial
government as a messenger and interpreter to Indians
in the region; presumably he learned both the Iroquois
and Delaware languages.

The reasons for and the actual date of his emigration
from Poland remain clouded. According to one account
transmitted in family files, however, Sadowski was
taken prisoner in the fighting in the Great Northern
War of 1700 when the Swedes invaded the continent.
Removed, half-dead, to a prison ship, the Pole managed
to escape and eventually made his way to the "Free
World" of America. He landed in New York (New
Amsterdam at the time) during the first decade of the
1700's. Another version of the story is that Sadowski
became a Protestant, suffered persecution in the

predominantly Catholic Poland, fled to Prussia, and then immigrated to the colonies.

Temporarily, Sadowski settled in what is now New Jersey. He married a first generation Hollander and set about to learn the new customs and language of his new world. Being by nature adventurous, restless, and daring, he was not content to remain in quiet backwater country when far-reaching lands, forests, rivers, and mountains beckoned him on. The lure of the unexplored path took him into Pennsylvania, traveling by foot, pack horse and canoe. He was struck by the beauty and fertility of the country and, in 1712, he bought four hunded acres of land for a reported thirty pounds along the Schuylkill River some fifty miles from Philadelphia. The tract was part of a large land grant to Swedes who had come to America; these settlers divided their grants and sold to new arrivals.

Under leadership of the Quaker, William Penn, Pennyslvania acquired a strong tradition of religious freedom, self-government, and friendship with the Indians. These considerations, coupled with the majesty of the site, completely won over the immigrant Pole. He constructed a rude hut on the tree-studded land before building a bigger homestead and began cultivating the acres suitable for fields and pastures. Sadowski, as an axe-bearing settler as well as an explorer, carved out a prosperous farm.

The transplanted Pole earned a reputation as a respected and active citizen and, in 1718, joined with some of his neighbors to form a township. An English Quaker, George Boone, who was to become the grandfather of Daniel Boone, surveyed the boundaries in preparation for township. Inhabitants chose to call their district, Amity, because it mirrored the peaceful relations they maintained with nearby Indians. The name of Sadowski already had appeared on different legal documents; he had witnessed a will, prepared an inventory of a citizen's estate, and helped to organize a Protestant church in the area where he lived.

All this activity suggests Sadowski had forsaken the call of the wilderness, but this was not so. His immense energy and strongly kindled interest in Indians led him to Indian villages and settlements within Pennsylvania and without; he turned these trips into trading journeys. The pattern of trade was to buy furs from the Indians and sell these overseas to buy supplies needed by the colonists. Sadowski followed Indian trails to develop new trading areas, first to the forks of the Susquehanna River and, later on, down the Allegheny, Ohio, and other rivers.

An early Americana collector's item, a reference work called *The American Pioneer* which consisted of sketches about the settlement of the country, reported in an early 1842 history that the Polish trader "established himself near the present site of Lower Sandusky, at the foot of the rapids of the river. His operations in trading for furs . . . with the Indians, being entirely confined to the river and bay, they soon became known to Europeans as Sanduski's river and bay."

During Sadowski's time the French watchfully guarded their stake in the New World and sought to confine the English to coastal regions; the French and British vied for the trade of the Ohio drainage area. In the face of growing tension between the two European powers, Sadowski found himself in a position to offer important intelligence to the English on what the French were up to. "While keeping up active trade with the Indians, who liked and trusted him," explained a direct descendant of Sadowski, "he learned from them the many moves made by the French to keep power over the territory between the Miami River and the Allegheny and even the Susquehanna. He passed on this information faithfully to the Penns and their successors." This was an accomplishment proudly stressed by Mrs. Ailene M. Williams of Urbana, Illinois, seventh in line of direct descent from Sadowski, who has accumulated extensive source and reference materials on her predecessor.

Sadowski was never an Indian fighter; he believed in gaining the trust and friendship of America's only natives. In times of trouble with Indians, he was called upon to try to make peace. When, in 1728, a group of Shawnees went on a rampage, Sadowski was commissioned by Governor Patrick Gordon of Pennsylvania as a messenger-interpreter to the Indians to try to arrange a peace meeting. He and other members of the peace party traveled with messages and gifts to chiefs of the tribes in the area where the Indians had stirred. Friendly contact was in time restored.

Describing the Indian unrest on the frontier during that period, Sadowski wrote a terse account to a fellow Indian trader in Philadelphia. He related, in highly original spelling, reflecting a tendency to put down English words according to Polish phonetics: ". . . the Sauanos (Shawnees) have hangd Thimity Higins (Timothy Higgins, an Indian trader at Malson, a town on the Susquehanna) upon pol (pole) of their cabin . . . & it is fierd (feared) that with the rest of the borders is not well . . . please acquint (acquaint) the Governor with seame (same) . . . the people in our parts is freed (afraid) that there is som miscif (some mischief hatching) by the Indians." Sadowski further reported that he himself had been warned not to go to the Indians in the fall on trading missions until better understanding had been achieved between the Christians and Indians because a great dissatisfaction had arisen between these groups. This letter has been preserved at the State Library and Museum at Harrisburg, Pennsylvania.

Conflicting stories exist as to how and when the intrepid pioneer died, one theory being that he was killed by Indians in Virginia. More exhaustive investigation has advanced the contention that he died peaceably in his home township and lies buried under a broken tombstone about a mile from his homestead. In recent years, a Sadowski Memorial Committee was formed with headquarters in Philadelphia to commemorate the deeds of the early explorer. An historical marker signed by the Pennsylvania Historical and Museum Commission was placed, in 1966, at Douglassville with this dedication: "Anthony Sadowski—Polish pioneer, Indian trader, settled along Schuylkill River in this area, 1712. He served the Provincial government as a messenger-interpreter during negotiations with Indian tribes in 1728. He was buried, 1736, in the graveyard of St. Gabriel's Church."

Before his death, Sadowski filed a will dated December 29, 1735. He mentioned several daughters but only one son, Andrew, and made careful disposition of all his worldly goods. In addition to his land and home, he left substantial livestock and crops of wheat and rye. His property included hundreds of household and farm items. The meticulous, handwritten testament evidenced Old Country script and the immigrant Pole signed his name with a flourish, using "Antoni," the correct Polish spelling. While no known portrait of

Sadowski exists, he is assumed to have been excep-
tionally sturdy and stalwart, with the endurance of a
soldier and the agility of an Indian.

Sadowski's son, Andrew, explored into Virginia and
eventually settled there. Andrew's offspring maintained the family tradition of pushing on toward new
frontiers and migrated to Kentucky. According to one
account, these Sadowskis joined the first surveying
party sent by the governor of Virginia to Kentucky to
plot out land for veterans of the French and Indian
War. They were delighted with the country and resolved to return. In the first volume of *The Winning
of the West,* a pioneer of Slavic ancestry called "Sowdowsky" is mentioned as the co-leader of some forty
men who founded Harrodsburg, Kentucky. These settlers built cabins and sowed corn in an effort to put
down a permanent settlement but the Indians came,
killed one of the group, and caused the rest to disperse.

"Sowdowsky" (this was Jacob Sadowski, who became recognized as a dedicated, methodical adventurer) and a companion decided not to return across
the mountains to safety in the face of the Indian threat.
Instead, they pierced the woods to the Cumberland
River where they built a canoe and descended down
the Mississippi River all the way to New Orleans. No
casual feat was this, for they were the first white men
to conquer this dangerous and untraveled route. From

New Orleans they took a ship to Virginia.

Jacob and a brother (probably James) joined the most famous of all pioneer heroes, Daniel Boone, on his perilous sallies into unchartered frontiers. Boone, about 1770, lived in Boonesborough, Kentucky, and probably knew more about Indians at that period than anyone in America. As longhunters and companions to Boone, the Sadowski brothers made their mark in Kentucky history.

The historian, Miecislaus Haiman, who has traced the Polish past in the United States most extensively, disputes the claim that the geographic name of Sandusky can be pinned down to an Anglicized version of Sadowski, but gives full credit to the family for a courageous contribution to the pioneer knowledge and growth of America. Anthony Sadowski, summarizes Haiman, "penetrated very early into Ohio as an Indian trader . . . and by the end of the eighteenth century, Sadowski and his descendants covered a large part of the middle west with pioneer traces."

In helping to blaze the way west, Anthony Sadowski and his progeny faced all possible threats from nature and man. They braved silent murder on trails by unseen enemies, captivity and torture at the hands of marauding Indians, fearsome attacks by herds of wild game, exposure to starvation and exhaustion and frightful storms. Always, they pushed forward in the shadow of the danger that the high mountains, deep forests, and quick-flowing rivers might hold them prisoner forever in their unmapped and unknown expanse. The Sadowskis belonged to those adventurers who not only relish the challenge of the untrod way but willingly seek it out.

First Lady of the Theater

Helena Modjeska

> "She passed like an angel upon the Polish firmament
> of art and genius, showing the lightning of it on two
> hemispheres."

DIFFERENT ANECDOTES DESCRIBED the compelling impact of the actress, Helena Modjeska, but none more vividly than the story of the prompter who, during Modjeska's first American performance of the very tragic *Camille,* threw away the script, retired to a dark corner behind the scenes, and had a good cry. This dramatic artist captivated audiences on two continents during the second half of the nineteenth century to become one of the most applauded theater personalities of all time. America adored her and she, it, for the Polish-born actress chose to live in the United States and died there, as a citizen.

Slim, graceful of figure, and noble in posture, Modjeska was not characterized as conventionally beautiful but, rather, as expressive, piquant, soulful. She possessed a voice of both sweetness and power, and excited rare empathy. That she performed in the United States in a language not her own and with an accent that became a kind of winsome accessory made her even more enchanting to American audiences. Modjeska herself revered acting and once declared: "To live in the imaginary world of my heroines, to speak their poetic language, to render different sentiments, to work out a character were the most cherished delights of my existence."

This "First Lady of the Theater" was born October 12, 1840, in the romantic and patrician city of Cracow, in the south of Poland. Legend suggests that she was the daughter of a prince, that her father was a member of a celebrated aristocratic family—and this may have been so. But she grew up, under the last name of Opid, within the circle of a large family and it was to her mother, the widow of a businessman, to whom she owed her upbringing. As a child, "Helcia"—the affectionate diminutive by which she was called—began to feel a sensitivity to the sweet melancholy that exists in many Polish songs and poems and her young companions took to regarding her as a "weeping willow." At seven, she saw her first play and was impressed for a lifetime.

The young Helena attended a convent school and

was tutored in music, art, and literature. She continued to see plays whenever possible and came to consider theaters as "temples" because, as she wrote years later in her memoirs, "they filled my being with a kind of rapturous awe." With other members of the family —she had talented half-brothers who came to some fame in the Polish theater—she took part in home theatricals. The maturing Helena thus lived in a world of half-fantasy and, while still very young, became enamored of her tutor, Gustav Sinnmayer Modrzejewski, who was much older than she. He had been a part of the family circle for many years and while a learned man, he had some aspects of an adventurer. The pair went to live in a small town outside Cracow where a son, Rudolphe, was born. There, in the provinces, the still stage-struck Helena began to act. Sinnmayer Modrzejewski organized a road company and became her manager. The year was 1861.

The ambitious actress stepped onto the stage under her theater name of Modrzejewska which she later was to simplify to Modjeska to accommodate American audiences. She gained immense popularity with the provincial public and the company prospered and grew, to a traveling component of twenty, and eventually thirty-six members.

"We started out," recalled the famous actress in her memoirs, "in a large, three-seater wagon covered with white canvas looking like a prairie schooner. We were as free as birds. . . ."

For some two years, she lived a vagabond existence, journeying from one small town to another, appearing in a variety of roles familiar to Polish theatergoers. In her domestic life, she looked to the upbringing of her son. A daughter, Marylka, was born a few hours after the mother-to-be appeared in a five-act tragedy; the child died, however, in 1865. Helena and Sinnmayer Modrzejewski visited Vienna in 1863 where she spent her time at the opera and theater, absorbing the sight, sound, and craft of some of the great names in European theater. The experience kindled ever stronger fire and inspiration for acting.

The liaison between Helena and her mentor was not destined to endure and the couple became estranged in 1865, after the death of their daughter. Some biographers characterize him as a Svengali, a domineering personality with an influence of evil, but even these concede that this erstwhile bewitcher was the creator of Helena as a professional actress. He had a natural talent for promotion and used it to best advantage in the theater. After leaving him, Helena returned to Cracow, obtained legal custody of their son, and devoted herself completely to perfecting her talent as an actress. She was quick to sense flaws or possible flaws in her professional development; she gave hours a day to improving her voice tone and volume.

Not long after she resettled in her hometown, she signed a contract with the Cracow Theater for a three-year engagement which came to establish her as a serious and accomplished performer. Her abilities were hailed by harsh and discerning critics and she moved into a cultured world of writers, composers, and artists who both applauded and admired her. During the summer of 1866, Helena met Count Karol Bozenta Chlapowski, an aristocrat of a sensitive and refined temperament who had a special taste for English poetry. After a two-year courtship, they were married, despite objections from some members of the titled Chlapowski family. The ceremony was performed at historic St. Anne's Catholic Church in Cracow and the pair took up residence in Warsaw.

These were years of dramatic insurrections in Poland and citizens throbbed with strife and patriotic fervor, chafing at every new demand and injury inflicted by occupying powers. In Warsaw the mood was at a high pitch. When Madame Chlapowska (the "a" ending designates a woman's surname) and her husband arrived in Warsaw, the temper of the capital mirrored intensely the not-to-be extinguished aspirations of the country for independence and a watchful patience in the vigil to advance toward the determining blow for freedom. Count Chlapowski was associated with a progressive paper called *Kraj* (*Country*) and was identified as a liberal. Difficulties with the Russian authorities, who controlled the capital, were bound to arise—and, in time, they did.

Although Warsaw residents inwardly bore their lack of freedom with sad hearts, they outwardly in day-to-day life sparkled with spirit, wit, and activity and swarmed to parks, squares, coffeehouses, clubs, and theaters. Provocative literary evenings, elegant dancing parties, and soirees sparked by the brilliant presence of the country's leading intellectuals provided a stimulating and enviable atmosphere. The Chlapowskis not only shared this life, they became a center of it, with their home transformed into a salon where the cultured world met.

Madame Chlapowska signed a contract with the Imperial Theater in Warsaw that made her the reigning actress of the nation at a salary reputed to equal that of the first minister of the Russian empire. She emerged the toast of the capital in a dazzling introductory performance in *Adrienne Lecouvreur,* a classic play about a beautiful and generous-hearted woman betrayed by the man to whom she gave her trust and love. Helena had her choice of roles at the theater and glittered as a luminous star on the Warsaw scene for seven years before political and social complications caused her to think of uprooting.

The Russian regime came to look suspiciously on the frequent gatherings under the Chlapowski roof, suggesting they had political connotations. The authorities also failed to appreciate the nationalistic views of the couple and their associates. And, in the theater, rumors and intrigues and jealousies arose, to such an extent that the famous actress asked herself: "Was it worthwhile to give all we had of the best of ourselves to the world, in order to obtain as a reward momentary applause followed by a cup of bitterness?" Apparently, her answer was negative, for she and her husband and a handful of close friends decided to set sail for America as colonists, smitten by the freedom, adventure, and opportunity they saw ahead. Willingly, the idolized Modrzejewska, who had continued to perform under her chosen theater name, gave up the crown as the leading actress of Poland.

The Chlapowskis began their long sea journey on July 13, 1876, from Bremen, the German seaport, and arrived more than two months later at their destination: California. They stopped in New York and proceeded to San Francisco by way of Panama. Their goal, however, still lay beyond; they headed for Anaheim, a town nestled in a charming valley at the foot of the Santa Ana range which was inhabited mostly by German colonists and Spaniards. It was located south of Los Angeles close to the Pacific; here the Chlapowskis and their fellow colonists hoped to live off the golden earth as farmers in a Utopian settlement. Why had they come to this particular location? Mostly, they had been influenced by the reports of a young writer and colleague, Henryk Sienkiewicz, who traveled ahead to scout out a settling place. This fellow Pole was a partner in the colonizing venture; his stay in the United States inspired his writing, which earned him the Nobel Prize for Literature in 1905, even to providing characters for his famous novel, *Quo Vadis?*.

Full of ideals and romanticism about their purpose and new setting, the Warsaw group moved into a rented ranch house and purchased an orange grove and vineyard. The colonists quickly learned that fruit farming was more than plucking succulent, sun-ripe products off trees and vines. Being intellectuals, they had no idea of the practical considerations in tilling the earth and made a sorry mess of the Utopian experiment. There were amusing as well as disastrous experiences, and the entire company languished in the misery of homesickness.

Madame Chlapowska concluded that nothing but more misery would come from continuation of the experiment in cooperative living and resolved that she must return to her beloved livelihood of the stage. She announced she was off to San Francisco to learn English and to seek a chance to perform in the theaters of America. Her husband, who had spent thousands of dollars of his own fortune to launch the ranch experiment, supported her decision.

So, at the age of thirty-seven, Pani Helena (Pani is the Polish word used in polite address to a woman) applied herself to conquering the formidable sounds of the English language. Every day she memorized one hundred new words, wrote pages of exercises, and recited constantly in the strange new cadence of phonetics. When she felt herself ready to plunge into the world of American theater, she committed several plays to memory and knocked at the door of the widely known California Theater in San Francisco. At first, she was turned away but, eventually, she won a tryout. This audition convinced the theater manager he had found a new star and he signed her to a contract. But, looking at the spelling of her professional name, he muttered: "Who on earth could read that? I fear you will be compelled to change your name, Madame." She modified it to Modjeska.

Her first theatrical appearance on American soil was on August 20, 1877, at the California Theater in the same play with which she had taken Warsaw by storm, *Adrienne Lecouvreur*. About the triumph of her debut, Sienkiewicz wrote for a Warsaw editor: "Oh, that was a victory, a victory unmatched in the history of Polish art. When she finished there was silence, as if the audience was unwilling to free itself at once from her spell. And then—it is hard to describe what happened. A veritable tempest of applause, of cries, of calls. The public, by nature cold, let itself go to an extent the journalists told me afterward they had never seen Americans do before, never seen such a display of enthusiasm . . ." This performance led to a two-year tour that took the actress to New York where she first appeared in December of the same year.

Pani Helena was a performer so absorbed in her characterization that she transported her audiences completely along with her. In the New York appearance, she carried a shoehorn onto the scene, thinking it was a fan, and the audience virtually failed to notice it. In Boston, on opening night, she accidentally fell through a door on an exit and the audience thought the unusual departure was part of the act. When she appeared in *Camille,* the press was unanimous in applauding her poetic handling of the ill-fated heroine, and Otis Skinner, the eminent thespian, claimed that her interpretation had a "fragrance" about it, that Modjeska was the rare soul who could turn the blackest ugliness into something fair, the greatest sin into holiness.

At the end of her American tour, she and the count visited Poland and, in 1880, they went to London where the actress was resolved to perform. She did appear there, in *Camille, Mary Stuart,* and eventually,

Shakespeare's *Romeo and Juliet*. And, again, she conquered. The critics forgot that here was a foreigner tackling their beloved Shakespeare and they showered her with praise. She spent the next few years in Poland and England, returning to the United States in 1882. America became the definite land of her adoption. The Chlapowskis established a home outside Santa Ana, California, called "Arden," which became their retreat.

In her native language, the actress had a repertory of more than one hundred roles. In English, there were about ten and she concentrated on becoming America's leading performer of Shakespeare. She introduced the Henrik Ibsen play, *A Doll's House,* to American audiences in 1883 under the title *Nora;* this was the first production of Ibsen in English. During some thirty years of touring the United States, she played different roles, including Ophelia, Rosalind, Cleopatra, Desdemona, Mary Stuart, and Juliet. Personally, she preferred Shakespearean parts. One of her dreams was to produce a Polish play in English in the United States but this ambition was not realized. In Europe, she appeared on the stage in Ireland and in Prague, Czechoslovakia, and won additional fans on the Continent.

There was no question but that the fascinating actress helped to stir in the United States a sprightly interest in things Polish. She sparkled as a representative of what could be contributed to the performing arts through a background of Polish education, training, and culture. She was asked to lecture as well as to appear in plays and at the World's Fair in Chicago in 1893, she was invited to speak in behalf of Poland and Polish women. Because of deprecating references to the Russian occupiers of her partitioned homeland, the actress was forbidden afterward to set foot on any Russian territory.

As a citizen and resident of the United States, Pani Helena publicly discussed and gave interviews on what she saw as the needs and failures of theater in America. She pleaded for an endowed theater in the country, independent of box office, that would keep the talents and energies of aspiring actors and actresses directed toward artistic and literary ideals and not ticket sales. She criticized the "star" system as leaving much to be desired, arguing that it limited the opportunity for beginners and cut them off from chances for real development and interpretation of roles. Many of her ideas did become realities in America, though much later.

About her feelings for America she was forthright. The immigrant actress had gained citizenship in the United States through the naturalization of her husband; this was possible under immigration laws in effect in the country at that time. Speaking for herself and the count, she once observed: "Both of us have become Americanized in many ways. The long years we spent in this country have exerted a great influence upon our way of looking at things. . . . We have become very sensitive to the grandeur of our adopted country, its possibilities dazzle us and its wonderful growth and progress excite our enthusiasm. This new love does not injure our old love for Poland. It only broadens our feelings and knowledge." She gathered a wide circle of friends among Poles who had immigrated to America and among native-born Americans, including outstanding literary figures such as Henry Wadsworth Longfellow and Eugene Field. The son of the actress studied engineering and emerged a leading bridge builder under his American name of Ralph Modjeski. He was the chief designer of the much admired San Francisco-Oakland Bay bridge, a seven-mile suspension structure finished in 1936.

The stage remained so consuming a passion for Pani Helena that she found it almost impossible to retire. Originally, this parting was scheduled in 1902. But she left the stage, finally, only in 1907. In 1905, a brilliant testimonial was held in her honor at the Metropolitan Opera which proved to be her farewell to New York. At this event, she philosophized: "In the end, it is not applause that is the greatest reward for an actor. It is the awareness that he or she will live in the hearts and memories of spectators." After retirement, she and her husband continued to make California their head-quarters. Here they lived simply but cheerfully on limited funds because the count, who had been a kind of business manager for his wife, was neither practical with funds nor basically money-minded. Also, the actress had been generous in donations to Polish causes and helped to finance, for example, the building of the Slowacki Theater in her hometown of Cracow. Pani Helena fell victim to chronic Bright's disease and died on April 8, 1909, at her small home on Bay Island at what is now Balboa, California.

Tributes in different parts of the United States memorialized this queen of the American stage, but the final pageant of death took place in Cracow where she was buried. In the effusive Polish tradition, the funeral oration was full of grandeur and poetry. The eulogy gave lofty testament to the talent of Helena Modjeska, proclaiming: ". . . She passed like an angel upon the Polish firmament of art and genius, showing the lightning of it on both hemispheres." On her tombstone this tribute was engraved: "By her art she elevated the mind and refreshed the heart. . . ."

As an artist and personality, Pani Helena left an indelible mark in Europe and the United States. While born with an inclination toward acting and the stage, it was dedication, determination, long hours of study and work, and a compassionate understanding of her characters that shaped and refined the art of the eminent actress. Actors, she had remarked, needed an irrepressible desire of expression, together with the riches of feeling that can be exposed to the world with good taste and control. As she herself articulately explained: "To get out of myself, to throw my whole soul into the assumed character, to lead its life, to be moved by its emotions, thrilled by its passions, to suffer or rejoice —in one word, to identify myself with it and reincarnate another soul and body, this became my ideal, the goal of all my aspirations, and at the same time, the enchantment and attraction of my work." Small wonder that she is remembered as one of the greatest actresses of all times.

Patriot, Pianist, Diplomat

Ignace Jan Paderewski

"He is a genius who happens to play the piano."

Tₕₑy CALLED him "Paderoosky" in America and he won the applause and affection of millions of citizens as an unmatched piano virtuoso, an ardent statesman for the freedom of Poland, and a generous-hearted, kind-spirited human being. Magnetic in talent, character, and appearance, this fabled Pole made countless tours of the United States and died on American soil. His mispronounced name (the proper pronunciation is Pa-de-REF-skee) drew farmers from the fields, schoolboys from the sandlot, and businessmen from their offices into concert halls to see and to hear him. But his influence and persuasiveness extended far beyond the concert stage; he reached leaders of the world in pleading for a free Poland. It must be credited largely to Paderewski's efforts that the fate of Poland became an official concern of the United States after World War I. Infrequently does a single life touch so many important and different realms of interest as did that of Poland's Titan. While Paderewski never yielded his Polish citizenship, in many ways he belonged to America.

The artist-statesman was born November 6, 1860, in a country village called Kurylowka in a region of undulating landscape, rich farming soil, and bountiful orchards. His mother, the daughter of a university professor, was very musical; his father, an administrator of estates, played the violin. When Ignace was only a few months old, his mother died and he and his sister, Antonina, grew up tended by their father and each other.

Already, at the age of three, Ignace was attracted to the piano, at first playing melodies with one finger and, at four years, using all fingers. At six, he had composed his first piece. The sensitive child was aroused to his country's sad plight when his father, a revolutionist in Russian-ruled Poland, was dragged away to prison for a year by the Cossacks. The event seared his memory and soul.

After being tutored at home, Ignace was sent to Poland's capital to obtain the best possible training in music. At twelve, he entered the famous Warsaw Conservatory of Music, walking the same corridors as had the youthful Chopin. During his teens, young Paderewski displayed a mischievous nature and bold temperament and these attributes, coupled with his effusive mane of red hair, earned for him the happy nickname of "Squirrel." He was a rebel, too. When he refused to give hours to required student orchestra rehearsals which he preferred to spend on his own daily musical studies, he was expelled from the Conservatory, and not once, but twice.

Upon the second expulsion, the ambitious student decided to launch a concert career. He and two fellow teen-agers, one a violinist and the other a cellist, concocted an enterprising scheme: They would barnstorm as musicians for a year, traveling all the way to Russia. While the experience proved a tremendous adventure, it was far from any professional coup and certainly not any financial success. In the end, the trio became a duo and Paderewski, penniless, hungry, and wearing newspapers under his clothing to keep warm in Siberian temperatures, was rescued by his father who sent him money to return to Poland from Russia.

Paderewski then was allowed to finish his studies at the Conservatory and he obtained his diploma in 1878. The school honored his talent and performance by appointing him pianoforte instructor at the Conservatory.

During his teaching days, Paderewski met a charming and beautiful girl named Antonina Korsak, a music student. In 1880, when he had turned twenty, they were married. They moved into a small apartment and lived very happily, making glowing plans for the future. To Antonina, it did not matter that her husband brought home only meager earnings as a piano teacher; she adored him. Paderewski felt himself blessed with gifts for which he had longed: A home, a personal life of his own, and someone who belonged to him.

But the time of contentment was short. One year after the marriage, Antonina was dead, leaving her young husband with an infant son. Paderewski's grief was long in passing and he tried as he could during his entire life to care for the surviving child. Before Antonina slipped into final unconsciousness, she made her husband promise to use some of her small inheritance money to continue his musical studies. He was true to this promise and went to Berlin for advanced courses in theory and composition. The infant was left in the temporary care of a solicitous grandmother.

About this time, Paderewski almost lost hope of becoming a successful pianist and turned more and more toward composition where he showed ability already recognized. When he went back to Warsaw, however, he was determined to embark on a career as a pianist.

The famous actress, Helena Modjeska, helped to launch the struggling pianist on a successful path to the concert stage. As one of the best known artists in the world, she had done much to remind the world there was such a place as Poland and she was anxious that other people with promise, especially Poles, be given a chance to shine. After meeting Paderewski in the Polish mountain resort near the Czechoslovakian border called Zakopane, the actress arranged a concert in Cracow at which she recited a few poems and Paderewski played the piano. Her name on the program was magic. With money earned from the concert, Paderewski went to Vienna to become part of an illustrous society of musicians and artists and, more importantly, a recognized pianist.

From 1887, his career advanced as a continuous triumph. He spent seven hours a day practicing, often torturing himself over one passage in this pursuit of perfection. He believed that, in making music, the summit of the mountain was always farther and farther away. He prepared more and more programs, adding concerto after concerto to his growing list. His engagements led him throughout Europe, to France, the Netherlands, Belgium, England. He attracted many friends, including musical greats like Charles Gounod, Camille Saint-Saens, Jules Massenet, and Cesar Franck. In London he played for Queen Victoria. Obviously, Paderewski was a success but not all critics were unanimous in praise; the eminent Bernard Shaw, the critic with the caustic pen, dismissed the Polish pianist in one review as "a harmonious blacksmith."

The financial rewards of his European appearances were important to Paderewski, not for himself but for his son. Alfred, while alert mentally, was not developing well physically. The boy showed weakness of the limbs that probably was a form of infantile paralysis. Doctors at that time were not able to diagnose the condition precisely and could do little to improve Alfred's state of health. But the father kept trying to find some remedy and some assistance for his son, before he surrendered to the decision that the boy would not walk. In Paris, Alfred was nursed and cared for by a family friend, the generous-hearted Madame Helena Gorska, who gave love and kindness to him.

In his professional career, the next step for Paderewski was to try his luck in the New World which, to European artists, represented a land of fantasy and legend and hopeful fame. Engaged for eighty concerts under the auspices of the House of Steinway, Paderewski landed on American shores in 1891. The performer was aghast at the demand that he play six concerts in one week; in Europe, there was sometimes not the opportunity for six concerts in one season! His debut was at Carnegie Hall, under the baton of the eminent conductor, Walter Damrosch, on November 17. The United States made a profound, if somewhat bewildering first impression on him, and he commented on the many evidences of interest and friendship shown toward him everywhere.

Critics acclaimed him from the start and audiences almost literally carried him triumphantly from the platform. He was heralded as a poet in possession of the keyboard and his performances were described with phrases such as "glittering brilliance of execution," "complete rhythmic awareness," and "outstanding re-creative originality." While possibly not the equal of some pianists in sheer technical brilliance, Paderewski far outshone any competitor in the power of his artistic vision and in the majestic stature of his playing. He showed such concentration, appeal, and penetration during his concerts that listeners who sat in front rows seemed hypnotized by the performer. His handsome, sensitive face, his chrysanthemum of thick, red hair, his courtly manner, his aura of broodiness, all made for an extravagantly romantic and mesmerizing stage appearance. Probably no pianist has ever captured the American imagination as he did, keeping his hold for more than thirty years.

During his American tours, Paderewski made more than music and money; he came to be welcomed into the circles of the artistic elite, the barons of wealth, and the homes of presidents and politicians. He became a total personality to America. Between his early tours,

Casimir Pulaski

Thaddeus Kosciuszko

Helena Modjeska at the
start of her career

Helena Modjeska as
Rosalind in *As You Like It*

Paderewski as a young man

Ignace Jan Paderewski

Matthew Nowicki

Courtesy of Albert Mayer

Arena building, Raleigh, North Carolina, designed by Nowicki

Joseph W. Molitor

RCA Records

Artur Rubinstein

Rubinstein rehearsing with an ensemble

RCA Records

Dr. Casimir Funk

John A. Gronouski

Edmund S. Muskie

Stan Musial with President John F. Kennedy

Paderewski spent time in Europe and composed an opera called *Manru,* a folk story of gypsies living in the Tatra Mountains that still is performed in Poland. He remained better known for his piano works, particularly the widely played "Minuet in G." His trips to Europe always reunited him with his son whose physical condition steadily worsened. In 1899, Paderewski married Madame Gorska who, in effect, had been a mother to Alfred. The three settled on an estate at Morges near Lausanne, Switzerland, by the shimmering waters of Lake Geneva and within view of famous Mount Blanc. Here, in the peaceful and healthful surroundings, Alfred spent his last days. He died in 1901, at the age of twenty and was buried in a Paris cemetery, near the tomb of Chopin.

Paderewski toured many different parts of the globe and his name and talent spread around the world like a rainbow. In addition to long years of touring the United States, he performed in Russia, Australia, New Zealand, Africa, and South America. From his 1904 sojourn in Australia, Paderewski brought back a parrot named Cockey Roberts who made it a habit of perching on his master's foot during practice sessions, exclaiming from time to time, "Oh Lord, how beautiful!" In his journeys, Paderewski spread good will for his native land and emerged a double hero, of art and of his country.

When, in 1910, Paderewski spoke the following words at a Chopin celebration in Lwow, he spoke very much his own feeling: "No man, however great, can stand above his nation, or beyond his nation. He is seed of her seed, a portion of her, blossom of her bearing, fruit of her ripening. . . ." With the advent of World War I, Paderewski saw a chance that Poland could emerge at last as an independent country and made the transition from musician to orator, statesman, and diplomat. In 1915, he had plans beyond a concert tour upon arrival in the United States. He was a man with a mission, determined to raise money for the starving people of Poland and to convince Americans and American officials that Poland deserved a physical resurrection. "Give me seed for this trampled, wasted land, bread for these starving!" he pleaded.

Paderewski traveled across the United States, giving three hundred speeches in all for the cause of an independent Poland. His powers of oratory came close to equalling his musical eloquency. He opened one widely-remembered speech in San Francisco with the winning words: "I come to speak to you of a nation which is not yours, in a language which is not mine. . . ." After his speeches, he played the haunting, nostalgic music of Chopin and moved his listeners with notes as well as words.

Through Paderewski's persistent and untiring

efforts, the case for Polish independence was placed before world public opinion and governments. Wrangling an introduction to Colonel Edward M. House, confidential adviser to President Woodrow Wilson, Paderewski irresistibly documented his appeal. The powerful political figure promised to try to help Poland. Later, Paderewski met President Wilson himself at a diplomatic dinner and was impressed immeasurably by the president as a scholar and statesman. In the close race of President Wilson for re-election in 1916, Paderewski effectively supported him, believing in what Wilson stood for and would do for the peace of the world. The Pole was very much heartened when, meeting with the president during the course of the war, Wilson assured him: "Not only your country, but all Europe needs a new order." During World War I, a group of 22,000 Polish-Americans volunteered for service; they were joined by European Poles to form some 100,000 men under the banner of the white eagle on the Polish flag.

On January 8, 1918, President Wilson outlined before Congress a fourteen-point program for the peace ahead. No other single person could take more credit for the thirteenth point than Paderewski. This recommendation read: "An independent Polish state should be erected which should include the territories inhabited by indisputably Polish populations, which should be assured a free and secure access to the sea, and whose political and economic independence and territorial integrity should be guaranteed by international covenant." The simple but dramatic statement represented even more of a success than Paderewski had dreamed.

The pianist-patriot had won such authority that, upon creation of the resurrected state, he was seen as the only man who possibly could head the first government of the reborn nation. Paderewski was named Prime Minister and Minister of Foreign Affairs and succeeded in Warsaw in forming a coalition ministry. He represented Poland in Paris where statesmen of the world gathered to write the peace treaty and to rearrange the borders of Europe. The gains he won were important ones and a tribute to his influence and persuasiveness. When, on June 28, 1919, Paderewski signed the Versailles Treaty on behalf of Poland, the assembly evidenced its approval with a round of applause.

But Paderewski's political career did not last too long. The chief of state, Marshal Jozef Pilsudski, proved an extremely difficult partner with whom to work and differences in their views, in time, could not be bridged. Paderewski wrestled with many trying situations in attempting to make national unity a reality in a country so long splintered and Poles being Poles, they were not the most pliable people to do business with politically. While Paderewski previously could smile about the established bit of humor asserting "Put two Poles together and you get two political parties," he found it disheartening to face the kernel of truth in the joke. In the end, he resigned under the too heavy and somewhat fruitless burden of the administrative office. He announced his withdrawal on December 5, 1919, and then quietly left Warsaw.

Paderewski returned to Switzerland and, in 1922, returned to concert life. Again, he walked out on the famous Carnegie Hall stage, almost thirty-one years to the day of his American debut there. Critics were hard put to find adequate words to describe the mature playing of this artist, who was so much more than a pianist. He sped across the United States on tour in his special Pullman car which already was a familiar sight in the country. Paderewski once more charmed audiences in many places and many countries. He toured France, Belgium, England, and Italy. At his first post-war recital in London, the whole audience arose as he entered and remained standing until he sat down at piano.

Almost until the end of his life at eighty years, Paderewski was part of the concert scene. In 1939, in Milwaukee, the music critic of *The Milwaukee Journal*, Richard S. Davis, wrote in a moving critique:

"The man was dressed in his own fashion—in the formality of courts where he has played for kings. He wore his low folded collar with the wide white tie. His long coat seemed part of him. . . . Bitterness and resentment were not in that face and their absence made it difficult to believe the apparent truth that the old man is now playing his piano because he must."

The fact was that Paderewski had to return to the concert stage to make a living; he had no money. While once considered the richest living musician in the world, he had given away nearly all of his fortune in the service of the war-hungry people of Europe and in the service of Poland. The catalog of his philanthrophies would fill a volume. The generous-spirited artist gave proceeds from concerts for unemployed musicians; that happened to be in London. In Paris, he appeared in recital for the benefit of the Jewish refugees from Germany. Individually, he helped hundreds of struggling artists and became the benefactor of a whole generation of brilliant pianists. In addition, he helped to organize and sponsor many musical competitions. One of Paderewski's extravagant contributions, but a patriotic and enduring donation, was construction of a monument in Cracow by a talented sculptor to commemorate the Polish victory over the Teutonic Knights at the famous battle of Grunwald, back in 1410.

The death of his wife in January, 1934, left a depressive void in Paderewski's life and he shunned the public spotlight for some two years. Then, he was heard again, in a motion picture about his career filmed outside London. During these years, he yet managed to keep in touch with political happenings in Poland and Europe. In 1939, Paderewski was at his Swiss estate when the news came that his native land once more was being laid waste by an invader: Nazi Germany had stormed Poland. He was named President of the World War II Polish National Council, an organization in exile, a year later. Paderewski proceeded to the United States, sailing into New York harbor in November of 1940.

The musician-statesman considered America a second home and he held his guest country in great esteem and deep attachment, lauding it for many qualities, among these "a vitality and freshness unlike anything I had ever known." He knew the country well and lived for a time on a ranch near Paso Robles, California. He left the concert stage after suffering a slight heart attack before an appearance in Madison Square Garden in New York in 1939. The end came on June 29, 1941, in his New York apartment.

At Paderewski's funeral in St. Patrick's Cathedral, thousands crowded inside and almost 35,000 lined the streets outside. A train took his body to Washington where it lay in state at the Polish Embassy and the president of the United States himself arranged for

Paderewski's burial. He was buried as a hero in Arlington Cemetery, to remain there until Poland again would be free and the body could be transferred to his native land.

The eminent musician, world-acclaimed patriot, and noted diplomat left a legion of devoted friends and admirers, people who felt the love for all humanity that radiated from him. Citizens in the United States, Switzerland, Italy, France, and England regarded him as "one of them" because they sensed that he sincerely was. Many called him the "heart" of Poland. Tributes to this famous Pole were numerous but it was Saint-Saens who so succinctly put it: "He is a genius who happens to play the piano," clearly indicating that his musicianship was by no means the only important reason for his uniqueness.

Universities, governments and institutions awarded him countless honors. He won the Order of the British Empire, the French Legion of Honor, honorary degrees from some ten universities, including Yale, Columbia, New York University, Glasgow, Cambridge, Cracow, and Oxford, and the Polish government's highest military distinction, the Cross of Virtuti Militari, along with the Polonia Restituta, the highest civilian award. Paderewski left his mortal earth consumed by two loves: Love of music and love of country. It is hard to judge to which he was more addicted.

He Explored the Vitamin

Casimir Funk

> "Funk's investigation created new interest in studies of nutrition and he must be put down as the father of vitamin therapy."

ALMOST EVERYONE KNOWS that vitamins are essential to life. The word itself has become a household expression. What person, young or old, has not been impressed by the need to get enough vitamins to maintain the health of the human system, from head to toe? Children grow up with constant admonitions: "Drink your milk," "Eat your spinach," and "Take your vitamins." Rather early, they learn that vitamins are found in foods and also are available in pills. Yet, how many of us know anything about the history of vitamins? Where does the word come from and what does it mean? Who was responsible for tracking down the elusive entity? The story of vitamins is mainly a twentieth-century development, made possible by dedicated

93

scientists who identified the different vitamins, explored them and defined the roles they play in the human body. The scientist more closely associated with the vitamin than others and who named the substance was a Pole, Dr. Casimir Funk, who died in Albany in November of 1967. He has gone down in the distinguished annals of science as the explorer of the vitamin and is referred to as the "father of vitamin therapy."

The eminent biochemist was born in Warsaw on February 23, 1884, the son of Dr. Jacques Funk, a brilliant dermatologist. His mother, Gustawa, who was from a cultured family of Warsaw, once had ambitions of being a doctor but she settled for marrying a doctor instead. Poland's capital then was ruled by the Russians, and Polish citizens, trained and skillful in the professions, very frequently were ordered to serve the occupying power in faraway places. Dr. Jacques Funk, after finishing his studies, drew orders to join the Russian army as a physician. The Russian-Turkish War was being fought at this time and the Warsaw doctor of Polish-Jewish background found himself in charge of a hospital for typhoid patients in Rumania. During this service, he contracted the disease, too, but recovered. When, finally, he returned to Warsaw, he established a practice as a leading skin specialist. At the age of twenty-six, he married and three children were born to the couple. Only Casimir survived.

Casimir, from birth, had a dislocation of the hip which caused his childhood to be different from that of other youngsters. The parents saw different doctors and tried different orthopedic means to right the deformity. When he was only four years old, Casimir was sent to a special center at Augsburg, Germany, for treatment. There, he learned German so thoroughly during a year's stay that he had to start again to learn Polish when he came back to Warsaw. Despite all the measures taken to remedy the congenital hip dislocation, Casimir walked with a slight limp all his life and consciousness of the deformity tended to make him introspective and a bit withdrawn.

The physical problem did not really dampen Casimir's boyhood activities and he avidly explored the libraries, parks, art galleries, and museums of Warsaw, usually in the company of his father. The father was mentor, tutor, healer, and companion to his young son; the mother has been described as quite domineering. Dr. Funk took Casimir on delightful excursions, invariably ending at one of the city's myriad, zestful, and warming coffeehouses for a nibble at very sweet, delicious Polish pastry. The taste of these mouthwatering concoctions, often spiced with nuts and honey and fruits and topped with cream, lingered in the enthusiasm and memory of young Casimir. These were happy times.

Until he was about eight years old, Casimir was

schooled at home and be began to read extensively. Charles Darwin, the controversial evolutionist, emerged as one of his earliest heroes and Casimir tried experiments in his own garden under the influence of the famous botanist. When he was ten years old, Casimir was admitted to a Russian government school but the program was not one to challenge his active and already original mind. He and a favorite school companion, maintained a busy extracurricular schedule of scientific experiments and personal observation in the world of nature lore; this was early training for the later career of Casimir. The youngster yearned for quicker, more progressive education and he was sent to a private school. At the age of sixteen, the parents decided that Casimir needed untrammeled vistas for learning; they arranged for his further schooling in Switzerland.

Casimir attended school in Geneva, taking special studies in zoology and botany. But his attention to classes proved fairly casual because he became absorbed in the life of the enchanting city and its cosmopolitan inhabitants gathered from different corners of the globe. Geneva's fascination for the young student easily can be understood: Set on a sparkling lake that shines like a polished sapphire, the city is set amid tiers of vineyards and surrounded by the stalwart and beautiful face of the Alps. History, culture, and internationalism bestowed upon the natural charm of the setting an engaging cloak of civilization. Added to these attractions was a certain air of intrigue contributed by the diverse collection of residents, erstwhile residents, and visitors on the spot. Casimir thoroughly enjoyed his school days here, even to overspending his allowance and getting into financial straits.

From Geneva, Casimir went to Berne, the quiet political capital of Switzerland, set on a plateau overlooking the white-capped peaks of the Bernese Oberland. He enrolled at the respected University of Berne to specialize in chemistry. During his university years, Casimir became expert in the Bernese adaptation of the Swiss-German dialect; this was no easy task since the dialect is harsh, only spoken and not ordinarily written, and has been compared to a throat disease. In time, Casimir transferred to the organic chemistry department which happened to be headed by a fellow Pole. In July, 1904, he passed his oral examination for his doctorate. He was just past twenty years old.

Discussing his future with his family, Casimir agreed on biochemistry, a discipline still in its infancy, as his chosen field. He went to Paris to study at the famous Pasteur Institute. Paris was a center of science and advanced in bacteriological work, and Casimir spent two years there. At twenty-one, he became subject to Russian military service but authorities excused him.

From France, the scholar went to Germany where he felt riled by Prussian arrogance. He worked as a biochemist at a municipal hospital in Wiesbaden where there were well-known alkaline springs. Then came London where Dr. Funk's work on vitamins began in earnest when he joined the Lister Institute of Preventive Medicine in 1910. Again, he had to acquire another language and to adapt to a new land and a different people. As a Pole, Dr. Funk felt somewhat foreign in Switzerland, France, and Germany; in England, he experienced more of an affinity for the people. The language was no problem; he mastered it quickly.

The discovery that certain foods could cure specific diseases launched the search that led, in time, to the identification and knowledge of vitamins. Already, it had been determined that scurvy, characterized by weakness, anemia, and spongy gums, struck many sailors but not those who sailed in areas where they had access to citrus fruits and juices. "Something" in the juices of oranges and lemons and limes was seen as the key to the cure and prevention of scurvy. In the nineteenth century, a Dutch scientist reported that beriberi, a disease leading to nervous disturbances and possible death, was caused by polished rice or rice with the outer layers removed.

Dr. Funk studied the causes of beriberi and proceeded to try to answer just why some diseases could be cured by certain foods. He began experiments with pigeons and found there was an important nutritional substance in the bran coating of rice that was not to be found in polished rice. A long series of experiments and tireless research finally yielded what he had sought: Isolation of that part of the rice bran capable of bringing back to health pigeons in his laboratory sick with a form of beriberi.

The Polish-born scientist drew the world's attention with his conclusion that the crystalline chemical he had isolated represented a substance essential to sustain life. He called the substance a "vitamine," coining the name from "vita," which means life in Latin, and "amine" which designates chemical compounds containing nitrogen. The final "e" was dropped from the name when it was found later that not all vitamins contain nitrogen.

"Vitamine" was introduced officially in a scientific article which Dr. Funk had published in the British *Journal of State Medicine* in July, 1912. He suggested there were many "vitamines," proposing, for the moment, at least four: One preventing beriberi, another preventing scurvy, still another preventing pellagra, and a fourth preventing rickets. (Pellagra brought skin rashes and certain nervous and mental symptoms, while rickets was marked by soft, deformed bones.) Dr.

Funk speculated that all these "vitamines" were distinct substances, probably nitrogenous in nature. While later research proved him not completely correct in some conclusions, he was accurate in saying that several distinct chemical substances were responsible for the cure of distinct food deficiency diseases. This emerged as a novel notion; the idea that a definite chemical material was capable of preventing a disease helped to change the thinking of the times.

The material Dr. Funk prepared was the world's first pure vitamin and led directly to Vitamin B-1 or thiamine. He made evident that by removing the outer layer of the rice kernel, in polishing or refining it, the thiamine content was lost. This simple finding greatly reduced beriberi in those Asian countries where the diet consisted mostly of polished rice; the populations switched back to the traditional "primitive" but healthier fare of natural rice.

Dr. Funk encountered some difficulties in getting the concept of vitamins accepted. Medical experts countered that it was a lack of an essential amino acid or protein in polished rice that caused beriberi and similar scourges. This encouraged Dr. Funk to a new series of experiments that proved the cause of beriberi was not the lack of this protein. He proceeded to important problems of nutrition and asked vital questions about milk, even coming to an estimate of its general vitamin content. Very early, Dr. Funk asserted that vitamins in foods could have a close relationship to glands of internal secretion. He worked with fish oils, particularly cod liver oil, to show their benefits and the effectiveness of their concentrates in children. Dr. Funk helped to launch generations of American children on cod liver oil as a guarantee of health.

It was a Johns Hopkins University professor who most aptly characterized Dr. Funk's record of achievement by declaring: "Funk's investigation created new interest in studies of nutrition and he must be put down as the father of vitamin therapy." With the assistance of his father, Dr. Funk prepared a book on the subject of vitamins, discussing the nutritional needs of lower plants and animals. Many of his concepts became recognized and practiced in later years, especially in the United States.

In 1915, Dr. Funk first came to America to do research at the Cornell Medical College. He was restless in England and convinced that the future of a researcher looked brightest in the United States. He arrived with his wife, who was Belgian. Dr. Funk at last felt completely at home in a new country and decided to stay. The Funks moved to New York where their son, Ian, was born; he later became a physician and settled in Albany. Dr. Funk worked for different companies in the chemical industry, including H. A. Metz & Company, doing as much pure research as he could. He became an American citizen in 1920.

Three years later, Dr. Funk returned to Poland to head the State Institute of Hygiene at Warsaw. It presented a challenging opportunity and after struggling with inadequate equipment, lack of housing, and other difficulties, Dr. Funk organized the Institute into an operative concern. He advanced into interesting experimentation in the field of hormones. He began to define some of the chemical properties of hormones and reported, for one thing, that two hormones were secreted from the posterior lobe of the pituitary. On a very small scale, the Institute isolated and distributed the hormone, insulin. Dr. Funk left Warsaw in 1927 with an expanded record of achievement and an addition to the family; a daughter, Doriane, was born in 1924. At this period in Poland's history, political stability was hard to attain and Dr. Funk departed, personally convinced that this stability would not come.

The next stop for the biochemist was Paris where he continued his research by studies of sex hormones. He left France with his family in 1939, fleeing in the face of the approaching Nazi army. He had to abandon a laboratory housing valuable apparatus and chemicals and an experimental farm consisting of hundreds of rats, mice, guinea pigs, and turkeys at Bordeaux.

Already, in 1936, Dr. Funk had become a research

consultant to the United States Vitamin Corporation in New York, now known as the USV Pharmaceutical Corporation. Returning to America, he went to work in the laboratories of the company to develop theories, voiced before, on the nutritional interrelationship of vitamins and minerals to health; this led to preparation of different commercial products, particularly vitamin-mineral combinations. In 1947, Dr. Funk set up the Funk Foundation for Medical Research to pursue, in particular, the investigation of cancer. As early as 1916, cancer had interested the researcher and he presented a paper in that year that suggested tumors were propagated by unstable chemical substances, possibly a metabolic disease. Later, he and his associates did extensive work on the effect of hormonal factors on the growth of a transplanted tumor.

In his personality, Dr. Funk was quiet and diffident. All his life he appreciated those who were original and sensitive and wanted to create or discover—this spirit in a fellow being or scientist immediately endeared a person to Dr. Funk. He stood below middle height, somewhat thin, with rather a gentle face set with blue eyes. He remained vigorous throughout his life. His preoccupation with science and his work made him a non-joiner; he was not active in organizations or in social doings. Dr. Funk preferred to remain aloof from the public spotlight and was well known as a person only to his family and chosen close friends. While various Polish groups saluted him for his work as a scientist, he shied away from joining movements of only one goal or purpose. The Polish-born scientist, however, was quick to go to the defense of Poland in discussion and conversation. Basically, though, Dr. Funk was an internationalist. He held memberships in scientific groups and appeared in *Who's Who in America.*

While never a scientist to seek attention, Dr. Funk, nonetheless, received it. His work on vitamins has assured him a place among the lauded researchers of the world. With his death, an eminent contributor to the better health of people everywhere was lost.

Poet and Philosopher of Form

Matthew Nowicki

> "Nowicki more surely than any of his contemporaries
> bore within him the seed of a new age . . . that which
> he left undone through his death must now call forth
> the creative efforts of a whole generation."

ORDINARILY, ARCHITECTS do not command the serious
attention of their colleagues or the world before they
have given long and productive years to their craft.
But Polish-born Matthew Nowicki (pronounced No-
VEET-skee) must be put down as a rare architect who
established a niche by the time he was forty when,
tragically, his life ended. His work showed not only
greatness but his potentialities for future accomplishment were seen as almost the brightest of any rising
young architect. At least one building on the American
scene, the Arena at the State Fair in Raleigh, North
Carolina, assures Nowicki's place as a creator of new
form. This unusual structure, described as "a building

that sings," tied for tenth place in a survey of America's most significant buildings in the last one hundred years. A legacy of sketches, drawings, and designs, along with some brilliant papers on the nature of architecture, sustain Nowicki's genius. As head of the architecture department of the school of design at North Carolina State College, Nowicki made an inspiring impact on the students and the curriculum. At that time, the transplanted Pole was on his way to American citizenship; his first papers had been taken out the spring before his death in 1950.

Born on June 26, 1910, Nowicki was a member of an established Polish family. While the Nowickis lived in Warsaw, they also were close to the soil and rural Poland because the father headed the Agrarian Party for many years. Earlier he served as a legal consul in areas as distant as Siberia, where Matthew (Maciej, in Polish) was born. The father's professional duties also took the family to Chicago so that young Matthew spent some adolescent years acquiring a knowledge of English and some familiarity with the friendly and disarming ways of Americans.

Enrolling at the famous Warsaw Polytechnic in 1929, Nowicki gravitated toward drawing rather than architecture itself and the school, although affiliated to engineering more than to fine arts, gave him wide scope for his talents. Here, sketching and drawing were

used to make students aware of the nature of their surroundings, teaching them to see their environment as
structures. Drawings, with the main lines of structure
exposed, served as a means for exact analysis, both
visual and mental. This training endowed Nowicki
with an immense skill with pen and pencil and, later in
life, he translated his ideas in architecture through
quick, precise and inspired strokes of the hand. Architects with whom Nowicki worked in the United States
recalled that he could draw incredibly good sketches at
the rate of five minutes apiece.

Nowicki met his future wife at the Polytechnic; she,
too, was talented and a bright future in architecture
was predicted for her. During his years as a student,
Nowicki traveled widely and sketched as he journeyed
over most of Europe. As part of his learning, he had
the entire architectural richness of the Continent for
reference. The curriculum at the Warsaw school provided a beneficial mixture of traditional architecture,
the humanities, and engineering with its technical
methodology. Students also were influenced by new
leaders and ideas in architecture, and Le Corbusier,
the Swiss-born architect who made his home in Paris,
became Nowicki's temporary idol.

His start in architecture came in the same year as his
graduation, 1936. He was named an associate professor
of architecture at his own Polytechnic. It was an im-

portant year, for Nowicki also was married in 1936. In architecture, as well as in life, the Polish couple formed a close partnership. Establishing a private practice, Nowicki won prizes in competitions for office buildings, housing units, churches, and a pavilion for the World's Fair in New York in 1939.

When World War II broke out with the invasion of Poland by Nazi Germany, Nowicki was a lieutenant on training maneuvers, in charge of an antiaircraft battery. Even when spotting the waves of German bombers overhead directed toward Warsaw, he found it almost impossible to believe the onslaught had begun. In the devastation that followed, he managed to get back to the capital. During the occupation, Nowicki shared the terror and hardship of life in Warsaw. Secretly, he conducted underground classes in architecture and town planning (the Nazis banned such activities) while, officially, he taught bricklaying in a trade school that was permitted to be in operation. Participant in a siege of guerrilla fighting in the woods around Warsaw, Nowicki was forced to flee, together with his wife and their small son, who was born during the occupation. They went to a faraway mountain region near Zakopane.

One of the haunting memories harbored by Nowicki from his wartime days in Warsaw centered on a settlement for the blind called Laski, not far from the capital. He came across the center while on duty between Warsaw and the Kampinos Forest during the Warsaw Uprising of 1944 when the Poles openly revolted against the Nazis and suffered unspeakable losses. Compassionately, he considered the fate of blind people and shortly before the end of the uprising, he went to live among the blind and worked out building plans for them. Nowicki had a special goal: He wanted to create beautiful forms and buildings protected against rain and sun for the inhabitants. He envisaged different toned bells mounted on each building, bells that would be swayed by the wind, to supply pleasant sounds and not noises. He sketched architectural solutions to make everyday living for the blind easier, using a concept of small spaces to make every corner of an area familiar to the non-seeing eye. As it turned out, there was no opportunity to implement most of his ideas but Nowicki here clearly indicated how he put human considerations above all else in architecture.

At the end of the war, Nowicki prepared the plan for rebuilding the central area of Warsaw, left some 85 per cent destroyed. He conceived the idea of using the dismaying heaps of rubble in the ruined capital by placing buildings on a mound formed by this very rubble. When the chance came to go to the United States as technical adviser to the Polish Embassy, he seized it in order to enlist American aid in rebuilding

Warsaw. He worked first in Chicago and then at the United Nations where he represented the Polish government in the choice of a site for the permanent headquarters. Nowicki became the inevitable choice of Poland for the United Nations Board of Design and joined a high-powered, modern group of diverse architects. As the youngest member of the distinguished group, Nowicki did not influence in any significant way the plan for the building of the United Nations. But he absorbed valuable lessons that he was to remember years later in working out designs for the new city of Chandigarh, the capital of Punjab, India.

Nowicki's services to the United Nations gave him the occasion and means to cut off official relations with Poland and to begin a new career as architect and educator. The Communist coup in his native land made him fretful of Poland's future and he himself was too profoundly committed to freedom to accept any repression. Nowicki chose to be a part of America. He appreciated the United States for many virtues, but foremost for its democratic manners, social equality, a spectrum of differences, and the spirit of adventure. There was a chance for him in architecture, for America, too, was a land of change and innovation. Already, the architect was aware of all new developments and activities in his chosen field in the United States. In 1947, when Nowicki visited "Taliesin" at

Spring Green, Wisconsin, the inspiring architectural center of the world-known Frank Lloyd Wright, he was overwhelmed by the building, of which he knew all details.

Called to the School of Design at North Carolina State College in 1948, Nowicki plunged into an elaboration of his ideas to unite architecture with landscape design and city planning. He proposed an integrated curriculum that included descriptive drawing, structures and humanities and history. Although his ideas never were implemented fully, they basically aimed at an ambitious goal: Describing civilization in terms of architecture.

The creed of his teaching, as well as his architecture, sprang not from abstract theories or principles but from the needs of man himself. The high standards Nowicki demanded of his students he demanded of himself and although he asked both discipline and dedication, he was able to inspire it by his deep sense of duty, warm concern for others, and equitable temperament. While profoundly knowledgeable and brilliant, Nowicki valued the thoughts and opinions of others, whether those of a student, charwoman, eminent architect, or a peasant in India. He remained a simple human being, understanding and tolerant, and full of optimism.

The best example of his applied talents came out in

North Carolina, in a project which associated him with
William H. Deitrick in the design of buildings and
grounds of the State Fair at Raleigh. Though modern
architecture was not an obvious element in the life of
the state, Nowicki won over officials at the State Fair on
an Arena structure at once bold, imaginative, and daring. In his approach, Nowicki showed an audacious-
ness that America had brought out in him. He settled
on a design of two gigantic parabolic concrete arches,
intersecting close to the ground, to support the roof
and to frame the grandstands. One architectural critic
suggests that the arches "are like athletes who grasp
each other by their hands as they lean outward over the
circus-like arena. . . ." A startling design, it prompted
startling approval. The structure had both freshness
and beauty.

While teaching, designing the State Fair buildings,
and working out other concepts, Nowicki started a
project that was to draw fully on his powers. As consultant with the New York firm of Mayer, Whittlesey &
Glass, he embarked on designing the new capital of
Punjab in India. The project represented both a
magnificent opportunity and awesome task; the de-
signers would summon an entire city to life on a plain
at the foothills of the Himalayas—an ideal city, possibly a perfect city. Upon arriving in India, the country itself, with its sharp contrast of wealth and poverty,

shocked Nowicki. But he remained open-minded and the Hindu culture, with its rich buildings, ornament, and symbolism, impressed him. He was ready to learn from a new environment and new experiences. With his quick intuitive perception, Nowicki assimilated the spirit of the culture and worked to produce designs in harmony with local tradition.

Main decisions about the plan of Chandigarh were made before Nowicki and Albert Mayer, of the New York firm, an outstanding architect and city planner, arrived in Punjab. Here they encountered trying circumstances and conditions. They had expected to engage in serious work but discovered that the Indian bureaus had done nothing to prepare for the project or them; there was no staff, no drafting room, no accommodations. Instead of working out the design of the Capitol buildings and great city squares, as he had anticipated, Nowicki had to settle for designing small houses and planning a superblock. But he showed no disappointment and took to the job devotedly and gaily. He spent the next six weeks alone, working in an isolated hill station called Simla. Mayer, upon rejoining Nowicki, was astounded at the quantity of work produced—drawings "full of gaity, almost as a cartoonist's drawings are" and "the flow of imagination through it all, as though the work and thinking had been quite unhurried, quite undistracted by the other complications of the Punjab situation," as Mayer described it. Nowicki, meanwhile, also had worked to iron out the local issues and political problems holding up the project, showing impressive skill and tact in his efforts.

The low-cost living quarters Nowicki proposed for the new Indian city took into account the social habits of the poor villagers, the intensely hot summers, the searing winds, and the need for some familiar ornamentation. He deliberately ignored the customary solution to quick mass housing in this part of the world —long strings of white stucco flats. Instead, he designed a row house, small because the people were poor, using locally made brick and with textures recalling the intricate ornamentation of the Hindu house. At the heart of the row house was an inner courtyard to give refuge from heat, winds, and glare. Mayer considered this solution "a gem in architectural scale and feeling."

The Polish-born architect and city planner carefully had thought out the meaning and functions of a city, a topic which city fathers and builders wrestle with to this day. He divided the life of the city into two functions, an everyday role and an occasional or "holiday" role. Philosophically, Nowicki explained: "The everyday function—working and dwelling—is responsible for the pattern texture of the city plan. The holiday function is responsible for the basic conception of the great scale composition. The holiday function unites the city. . . ." In all his work, Nowicki stressed a need for logic and economy, declaring that "the concepts of economy and beauty derive from the same source; the utmost economy is the utmost beauty. This is the only surviving human appraisal of beauty."

For Chandigarh, Nowicki produced a sketch-design termed "the leaf plan," with the overall scheme based on the organic structure of a leaf. The stem became a commercial axis cutting the center of the city and branching into a veinlike system of traffic arteries; the Capitol building complex was at the top; the university was located to the west and an industrial area was placed at the opposite corner of the city. Within the Capitol complex, Nowicki sought to give the legislative building prominence by placing it atop a crowning shape of a necessarily larger secretariat.

Indian officials were so favorably impressed by Nowicki, both as a planner and a person, that they sought to retain him to guide the architectural development of the new city, serving directly as an employee of the Indian government. The contract between the Indian government and the New York firm covered the master plan only, and the Indians needed an overall development director.

While still engaged on the project, Nowicki planned

to return to the United States to settle some pending commitments. He traveled by way of central India to see some famous ruins and then proceeded to Bombay to catch a flight to the United States. The TWA Constellation in which he was traveling never reached New York. It crashed about sixty-five miles north of Cairo, Egypt, of a cause not determined. All fifty-five persons aboard were killed. The date was August 31, 1950.

The further tragedy was that Nowicki's sensitive and original designs and plans for Chandigarh never were executed. His death prompted selection of a new architect and a second team; the assignment shifted to a French and British team because the Indians decided payment should be made on a pound sterling basis. Le Corbusier and his associates took over the project in 1951 and the realization of Chandigarh became almost a virtuoso performance for the Paris-based architect. While the city contained elements of the original master plan, the lightness and livability with which Nowicki had hoped to endow it, fell, neglected. As finally constructed, the city emerged, according to some critics, as more sculpture than architecture, more monument than any human living environment.

There is no question but that Nowicki, by his compelling personality, his energy and persuasiveness, his friendliness and tact, did much to keep the Chandigarh project alive during the extremely difficult days of confusion and political turmoil. There also seems to be no question that had he lived to see the finish of the notable project, Nowicki would have turned out a city both humanely oriented and genuinely experimental in methods of architecture, a new architecture yet to be born.

Nowicki's performance, while limited, was unique. Altogether, he was on the American scene for four years, beginning in 1945. Yet he left an extraordinary impact. His colleagues in the profession remember his fecundity, freshness, and variety of ideas in architecture. His friends dwell upon his warm humanity, his intense articulation of concepts, his affability, his sense of order and harmony, his joyousness. A hulking figure, Nowicki stood more than six feet tall, with a long face that bespoke inner repose and kindness. He reflected on the needs of people everywhere and one of his ideas for America was that specialists in the professions, human relations, and teaching should be sent abroad for a period of several years to help the United States in its world mission. These should be men of high caliber and enthusiasm who themselves would be gaining from the experience of working abroad, Nowicki suggested. Does this idea not seem like a forerunner to the Peace Corps? Those who knew Nowicki best, loved him best and his death was a savage blow to his wife and two sons. Mrs. Nowicki is professor of architecture at the University of Pennsylvania and a dedicated, brilliant educator.

It is not surprising that outstanding American architects with whom Nowicki had worked, figures like Eero Saarinen, Wallace K. Harrison, and Albert Mayer, showered him with plaudits. Saarinen, who asked Nowicki, in 1949, to collaborate with him on a series of buildings for Brandeis University, made this observation: "If time had allowed his genius to spread its wings in full, this poet-philosopher of form would have influenced the whole course of architecture as profoundly as he inspired his friends." Mayer, Nowicki's very close friend and colleague, declared: "Matthew was not merely original, merely bold, merely an innovator, but an architect whose work was organically connected with the greatest contributions of all architectural time." Harrison pinpointed Nowicki as "a great architect and a most gifted designer."

Possibly the eminent American critic, Lewis Mumford, best summarized the scope and promise of Nowicki. Mumford said: "Nowicki more surely than any of his contemporaries bore within him the seed of a new age . . . that which he left undone through his death must now call forth the creative efforts of a whole generation."

Musician of Grand Design

Artur Rubinstein

"His colleagues consider him a miracle . . . and nobody will put up much of an argument when he is called the greatest living pianist."

R ARELY DOES a performing artist become a legend in his own time. But Artur Rubinstein, whose career already has spanned more than seven decades, who has played more concerts before more people than any other artist, who has sold more record albums, grossed more money, and attracted the widest popular following of any classical instrumentalist in history, must be set down as a living legend. Often called the complete artist, the Polish-born virtuoso represents as well the complete man, for not only does his remarkable musical talent but his whole exuberant manner of living mark him as extraordinary. Rubinstein treats life in the same way he approaches the piano—with taste, grace, and passion.

An American citizen since 1946, the pianist lives in Manhattan when not spending part of the year in Paris or on whirlwind concert trips. Interviewed to a point where he is almost public property, Rubinstein is known to even non-musical readers in the United States for his cosmopolitan tastes in foods, wines, and cigars; his delightful gift for conversation and story-telling; his encyclopedic knowledge of languages, books, and art. Recognized as the world's leading interpreter of Chopin, he belongs to that distinguished class of pianists encompassing Franz Liszt and Ignace Jan Paderewski.

At the precocious age of four, the virtuoso-to-be made his first public appearance, playing at a charity concert, and became the talk of his hometown. He was born January 28, 1886, in Lodz, a textile center in the north central part of Poland, west of Warsaw. The son of moderately prosperous Polish Jews (the father owned a hand-loom factory), young Artur showed uncanny comprehension of music as a toddler. He listened to his sisters' piano lessons and, by the time he was three, he could crawl up on the piano bench and play whatever he had heard them struggle through. He himself was assured of his future because, as a youngster, he passed out engraved cards on which was written: "Artur the Great Piano Virtuoso."

As a child prodigy, he studied under the best local

piano teacher in Lodz before going to Berlin as a "Wunderkind." There, he studied with the foremost teacher, Karl Heinrich Barth, who had been a pupil of Liszt and other great pianists. The young Rubinstein made his formal debut in Berlin three years later, and gave recitals in other German cities. In all, he spent some eight years studying in Berlin and recalled: "When Barth became angry, his little beard would rise until it practically pointed at me, and I would be terrified." Thanks to the efforts of an American music critic who heard Rubinstein play for Paderewski in Switzerland, the young pianist was invited to appear in the United States. He made an American debut at Carnegie Hall on January 8, 1906.

There were some favorable reviews by critics and the public applauded him, but he was no sensational success. One reviewer dismissed Rubinstein as "half-baked, not a prodigy, not an adult." The disappointed pianist went back to Europe to face some lean days, when he managed to keep one jump ahead of starvation by teaching piano to a succession of bright children in London. The times were so hard and bleak that Rubinstein, according to one story, even tried suicide but, fortunately, the belt he used for the deed snapped under his weight.

With time, Rubinstein gained a certain reputation as a pianist with fire and dash, a kind of musical showman, and he was content to live from this ephemeral pedestal. He drifted into continental life, spent time with artists and pseudo-artists and, by 1914, Rubinstein was turning more into a playboy and happy-go-lucky Bohemian than a serious musician. But, with the outbreak of World War I, he tried to enlist in the fighting unit known as the Polish Legion. Military authorities determined, however, that he would be more useful as an interpreter than a soldier. Under auspices of the Allied Army, Rubinstein also made a wartime concert tour in Europe.

A tour of Spain increased his popularity; his intensely vivid treatment of Spanish music captivated audiences. This new success made it possible for him to go to Latin America where Mexicans carried him through the streets on their shoulders. Rubinstein took the stirring, rhythmic works of modern Spanish composers like Manuel de Falla, Enrique Granados and Isaac Albeniz, wherever his tours led him. He popularized not only Spanish composers but young French and Polish writers of music as well.

In 1919, Rubinstein again appeared in the United States. Once more, critics were sparing in their praise, suggesting he dropped too many notes.

Returning to Paris in 1920, Rubinstein had renewed zest for the carefree, gadabout life of a bachelor and celebrity. He was a happy companion to artists and intellectuals, hobnobbed with greats like Jean Cocteau and Pablo Picasso and crisscrossed Europe, charming friends in many languages. He characterized himself as "an unfinished pianist who played with dash" and continued, at least, to please listeners.

In July, 1932, Rubinstein married Aniela (friends called her Nela) Mlynarski, the young daughter of an eminent Polish conductor, in a London wedding. He had met the honey-blonde beauty several years previously when he gave a concert in Warsaw. Rubinstein first became acquainted with the father at the turn of the century. Marriage and the birth of a daughter a year later prompted a new sense of responsibility in Rubinstein. In 1934, he retreated to a French Alpine village to bring a stronger discipline and maturity to his piano-playing. As he explained: "I didn't want people telling my child after I died, 'What a pianist your father might have been!' " Rubinstein converted a windowless garage into his studio and practiced six to nine hours a day perfecting his technique and repertory. New meanings and new qualities to music he had been performing for more than thirty years evolved. The artist who emerged from the candlelit garage set out immediately to establish a new audience for himself in Europe.

Now, Rubinstein felt ready to make another attempt to capture American critics and listeners; his third, and

successful, try came in 1937. Sol Hurok, the famous
impresario, was his sponsor. This tour brought him
rave notices in the United States and concert managers
soon offered Rubinstein twice his customary fee to
satisfy demands for appearances all over the country.
He was hailed as "a giant." Some critics suggested that
Rubinstein's failure to score a big success before this
time was because audiences in earlier years were not
yet ready for his advanced style. His manner, direct and
uncomplicated, for the most part, was too different
from the applauded pianists of the first decades of this
century who changed tempos and rhythms at whim and
lingered over emotional passages. Rubinstein's inter-
pretations then and later were unaffected, sane, poetic,
without excess mannerisms or gushy emotion.

In 1939, Rubinstein and his family moved from
Paris to New York and two of his four children were
born on American soil. He became an American citizen and later moved to Beverly Hills, California. As a
Californian, Rubinstein became movieland's *bon
vivant,* giving lavish parties, making gossip columns,
and taking part in delightful gags and jokes. Also, he
collected substantial paychecks for appearances and
dubbing piano scores in various films. While the Ru-
binsteins obviously enjoyed the climate and relaxed
way of life in California, they in time moved back to
New York because it represented a more convenient

American headquarters for them. They again set up a European home in Paris.

Rubinstein's genius and vast appeal as a pianist has been widely analyzed and written about. Partly, the incredible Rubinstein touch must be attributed to the physical structure of his hands, which are outsized. His little finger stretches longer than the middle finger of most people and with the extension of his long thumbs the reach of his hand on the keyboard covers a twelve-note spread. Most pianists are content if they can handle a tenth. In his chest, arms, and shoulders, Rubinstein boasts the strength of a professional wrestler. Then, there is the aura which the virtuoso radiates at performances, an aura which convinces listeners that the event they are attending is no mere exercise of a craft but a noble rite.

Anyone who has heard Rubinstein in concert can attest to the power and poetry of the occasion. The soloist appears with a brisk, decisive stride that conveys an urgent sense of high artistic mission. An inevitable storm of clapping greets the pianist, who responds politely by inclining his head gracefully. Then he sweeps back his coattails and takes his place at the piano. His profile (which Rubinstein once described rather aptly as "looking like a fish") is turned upward and he lapses into deep concentration. An intense expectancy builds up; when the hall is still and the last cough has died down, the hands of the master descend on the keyboard and the auditorium is filled with sounds shaped almost in the way a sculptor molds clay, surely and elegantly. Projected is the grand design of music and golden tones that are the envy of all pianists.

Rubinstein is astounding not only for his sumptuous tone and unfaltering technique but for his amazing quickness in memorizing scores and playing them with a marathon endurance. He used to average one hundred concerts a year and has been known to dash off feats like recording fifty-seven Chopin mazurkas in one sitting. His musical memory defies duplication. He can commit a sonata to memory in an hour and a well-known conductor declared: "Rubinstein is the only pianist you could wake up at midnight and ask to play any of the thirty-eight major piano concertos." In 1961, Rubinstein gave ten Carnegie Hall concerts in one season, an unmatched feat. The master pianist belittles his date-jammed calendar which he successfully manages even now that he has advanced into his eighties. "I lead a lazy life which most people call tremendously busy," he asserts. He does admit to nervousness before concerts and lists fear as the price he pays for his glorious life.

Possibly Rubinstein himself best explained his phenomenal success when he observed: "There has to be an element of daring in great music-making . . ." And his philosophy about music remains: "I like to win people's hearts." He traces his musical inspiration as proceeding from Brahms to Wagner to Tchaikovsky to Richard Strauss but all giving way to a more permanent infatuation for Schumann, Schubert, Mozart, and Chopin. He also has a high respect for modern music.

In appearance, the artist is stocky, dapper, and distinguished, carrying a weight of some 170 pounds on a five-foot, eight-inch frame. His complexion is pinkish, appropriate to his formerly ruddy hair, and his eyes are a blue described by different chroniclers as "gray-green blue" and "milky blue." His hair, now white, swirls about his dome like a curly halo. He tells many jokes about himself and his appearance. Once, when he was in a plane traveling between concerts, a flock of youngsters came to ask for his autograph. One boy returned a second time to say he could not read the name—how do you spell it? he wanted to know. Rubinstein asked why he did not ask one of the older children and the youngster replied: "They can't read, either." Then, why did they ask for his autograph? asked Rubinstein. "You look funny. You must be important," came the reply.

Philosopher, wit, conversationalist par excellence, aesthete—all of these describe Rubinstein. His gift for learning quickly has enabled him to soak up languages like sunshine. From colloquial English he can revert to fluent Polish and excellent French or to Russian, German, Spanish, Portuguese, or Italian. He owns some two thousand rare books and his collection of Impressionistic paintings would be a museum's joy. He chooses his wines with the knowledge of the highest French connoisseur and the foods he enjoys are drawn from exotic kitchens around the world. His friends are legion, and include presidents, queens, kings, artists, writers, scientists, composers, tycoons, and jet-set society. One of the most delightful tales involving Rubinstein also involves his friend, the mathematical genius, Albert Einstein. Once, the story goes, the two happened to be playing in a local impromptu chamber music group. Einstein missed a cue and came in four beats late. He was playing the violin and repeated the error. When it happened a third time, Rubinstein turned to Einstein and exclaimed: "Can't you even count up to four?"

Retaining the gallant manner and flowering traditions of the Old World, Rubinstein exemplifies the Renaissance man of deep knowledge and wide civilization. He is at home in Warsaw, Paris, London, New York, or Geneva, a citizen of the world. Though long ago he left his native Poland, he has remained a fervent Polish patriot and has contributed of his talent, time, and money to further Polish causes. He has been a judge in many of the Chopin competitions held in

Poland to discover promising young pianists and is respected and admired by Poles throughout the world. When, in 1945, he appeared in concert in San Francisco to mark the founding of the United Nations, he announced to his distinguished audience that, sadly, his native land (then under Nazi occupation) could not be represented. Then he sat down at the piano and gave Poland cultural and spiritual representation by playing with deep feeling and passion the Polish National Hymn which has a message that promises, "Poland is not yet lost. ..." Rubinstein's own family in Poland was wiped out by the Nazis.

Not just audiences but governments have paid tribute to the remarkable Rubinstein. Among his official decorations are the rosette of the Legion of Honor, presented personally to him by General Charles de Gaulle; the Polonia Restituta, the highest award of the Polish government; the Commander of Arts and Letters from Chile; the Alfonso el Sabio from Spain; and other awards from Belgium, Italy, and Portugal. While he is not much given to displaying his arsenal of honors, Rubinstein once was forced to wear them all because his children insisted on having at least one picture of him with all his decorations. The moment found Rubinstein resplendent but sheepish.

On the occasion of Rubinstein's seventy-fifth birthday, the music critic of *The New York Times,* Harold

C. Schonberg, summarized: "His colleagues considered him a miracle, geriatrics experts mumble when they talk about him, and nobody will put up much of an argument when he is called the greatest living pianist." And, on another occasion, a reviewer for the *Saturday Review,* declared: "If he doesn't play everything better than anybody, there are very few who play anything as well as he does."

Unbowed by age, the indefatigable virtuoso continues his fantastic career, still playing with the magical Rubinstein touch. He continues, too, his ebullient style of living in the bright, rosy-hued spirit of the irrepressible romantic. Rubinstein explains his immense zest by philosophizing: "Happiness really is only living, taking life on its own terms. I am passionately involved in life; I love its change, its color, its movement. To be alive, to be able to speak, to see, to walk, to have houses, music, paintings, it's all a miracle. I have adopted the technique of living life from miracle to miracle."

Edmund S. Muskie and John A. Gronouski

> "As poor boys, they early learned the sting of ethnic sniping, worked hard for their educations . . . then won high political office through pluck and luck rather than by any birthright."

MILLIONS OF AMERICANS stepped into election booths on November 5, 1968, to vote for the son of a Polish immigrant zoomed to fame as the Democratic nominee for the Vice-Presidency of the United States. Just months before, Edmund S. Muskie was unknown nationally. But, catapulted into the public spotlight as the running mate of presidential hopeful Hubert H. Humphrey, the lanky senator from Maine emerged the most refreshing and applauded figure from among all politicians seeking national support. In the traditional hurly-burly of campaigning, he won accolades for his appeal to reason, his disarming candor, his perceptive intelligence, his statesmanlike manner, his solid integrity. There was no storybook victory, however, because the Republicans won nationally; Muskie remained in the Senate, to face re-election in 1970. While this "Polish Yankee" caused an excited tinge of interest everywhere, he prompted an understandable ground swell of pride among Polish-Americans already aware of Muskie's achievement as the nation's first Polish-American senator and governor, of the traditionally Republican state of Maine.

The times had brought an era of ascendancy for Poles in politics, for John A. Gronouski also had splashed into the news headlines. In 1963, this Wisconsin-born educator and administrator attained the highest governmental rank of any Pole in the annals of America when the late President Kennedy named him Postmaster General of the United States. From this cabinet post, he moved into diplomacy, in 1965, as American ambassador to Poland, after nomination by President Johnson. When, in May of 1968, Gronouski resigned this high post to return to Washington to work actively in Vice-President Humphrey's campaign organization, the announcement caused no little shock. The departure involved principle over personal prestige. Ex-ambassador Gronouski stressed the duty he felt to participate directly in the very important process by which the United States chooses its highest executive. Quietly, he went to work behind the scenes for a party and candidates in which he strongly believed.

These two politicians of rank have much in common. Both grew up in nonaffluent circumstances, both struggled to get higher educations, both could recollect negative incidents associated with their ethnic background, both were determined to use their learning and talents toward the widest good, both have clung to their individuality. In themselves, Muskie and Gronouski underscore the continued reality of the American dream with its ideals of strong opportunity and many advantages. They can testify that the highest concepts of American democracy have not disappeared in the wake of protests, demonstrations, and disruptive violence. Possibly *Newsweek* magazine best characterized this genus of politicians in these words: "As poor boys, they early learned the sting of ethnic sniping, worked hard for their educations . . . then won high political office through pluck and luck rather than by any birthright."

It was James Reston, one of America's most respected political commentators, who wrote of Muskie in *The New York Times*: "He is the vice-presidential nominee of the Democratic party not because he comes from a big state, not because of his religion or his national origins—though these obviously help him politically—but because of his integrity." Integrity sprouts from beliefs and background, and for the six-foot, four-inch Democrat the story begins with an immigrant father who came to the United States from Jasionowka in Czarist-dominated Poland in 1903. The father, a tailor, fled conscription in the Czar's army. The family name was Marciszewski but when the immigrant, Stephen Marciszewski, successfully had negotiated the confusing entry formalities at Ellis Island, he had been dubbed with a shortened surname, Muskie. This name became official when the father took the oath as a naturalized citizen on August 5, 1912.

Senator Muskie was born in the mill town of Rumford, Maine, on March 28, 1914. His parents were so sure he was destined for distinction that they gave him the middle name of Sixtus, the name of five Popes. The senator was one of six children. His mother was Josephine Czarnecki, a native of Buffalo. Young Edmund attended Virginia Primary school in Oxford county and Stephens High School at Rumford. He was active in sports and debating and was graduated valedictorian of his class. As a youngster, he could remember the Ku Klux Klan burning crosses in Maine during the period after World War I in discrimination against foreigners and Catholics—people like the Muskies.

Muskie worked his way through Bates College by waiting on tables and washing dishes, won a Phi Beta Kappa key and other honors, including the distinction of being the "only Democrat on campus." On a scholarship, he attended Cornell University Law School and won a degree in 1939. He went to practice law in Waterville, Maine, but the war interrupted his career. Muskie spent some two years in the Navy as a junior officer on destroyer escorts in the Atlantic and Pacific. Upon his return to Waterville, he plunged into the world of politics, being elected to the Maine House of Representatives in 1946.

That was the beginning of the road that was to lead to national prominence. Muskie became minority leader of the small band of Democrats and served in the Maine House for six years. Eventually he was named Democratic national committeeman. Meanwhile, the eligible bachelor had strengthened his New England ties by marrying Jane Frances Gray, "the prettiest girl in Waterville," in 1948. One demand the groom exacted of his Republican bride: that she become a Democrat. Mrs. Muskie acquiesced and joined her husband in his political campaigning with delighted zest. The couple has five children, three girls and two boys.

Reluctantly, Muskie ran for governor in 1954 after nine other men declined the job. He launched a person-to-person campaign that took him 20,000 miles and into homes where voters had never laid eyes on a living Democrat. He won the race and became Maine's first Democratic governor in twenty years, as well as the nation's first Polish-American governor. Obviously, Maine voters liked him but then, too, there were many local and state economic problems that had gone unsolved over the years. Citizens were agreed on the need for a change. As governor, Muskie followed a non-partisan road, accommodating the Republicans in order to enact meaningful economic and educational programs. He was re-elected in 1956 and was tagged "the Miracle Man from Maine." During two terms, he helped to create a breed of independent voter known as the "Muskie Republican."

The Lincolnesque politician went to Washington in 1958 as the first popularly elected Democratic senator in Maine's history. His personal approach to politics, coupled with a lofty examination of crucial issues, won him friends and persistent voters. In the Senate, he became marked because of his monumental height and friendly, craggy good looks. A thoughtful legislator, Muskie has been described as having "the homespun charm of a Will Rogers, combined with a hard core of practical political wisdom."

As a freshman senator, Muskie, maintaining a stubborn independence, is reported to have crossed wills with the majority leader, Lyndon Johnson. Consequently, Muskie found himself serving on some obscure committees which he set out to make less obscure. He worked effectively and steadily to become an expert on air and water pollution and on federal-state relations. Muskie is called the father of air pollution legislation for his role in passing the Clean Air Act of 1963 and he led the fight for the 1965 Water Quality Act, a landmark federal law. As a second-term senator (he was handily re-elected in 1964), Muskie guided passage of Lyndon Johnson's Model Cities proposal. President Johnson has praised Muskie as "a real powerhouse . . . a match for Southern legislative craftsmen"; he is supposed to have considered Muskie as his 1964 running mate.

The tap to make the race for this office, however, came from Vice-President Humphrey during the Democratic National Convention of 1968. The honor was not one which the self-effacing senator actively sought. Notified of the decision, Muskie is reported to have blurted to his wife: "Mommy, I think we're stuck with it."

Once on the campaign trail, however, the Maine senator showed himself a master at commanding the serious thought and attention of all possible listeners. He seemed able to reach citizens and to have them accept his views, even though it was not what they might have wanted to hear. He told law enforcement officials: "You are not going to solve such problems as Vietnam and law and order and racial unrest with your emotion. You've got to solve them with your head." He told a group of milk producers worried about foreign milk products coming into the United States: "I do think we need certain adjustment devices to assure a stable market, but, no, I am not a protectionist." And in handling hecklers. Muskie far outshone other campaigners. Once, he countered interruptions from antiwar demonstrators by issuing a surprise invitation to speak to a twenty-one-year-old college student who shouted that young people never had the chance to talk in public. The heckler had his say, after which Muskie took to the microphone. And the student himself had to admit he was impressed with the candidate.

Whether the campaigning senator talked about the thorny problem of Vietnam or the history of hyphenated Americans or the hippie movement or the preservation of America as an open society, he made sense. The concensus seemed to be that the vice-presidential candidate traveled an uncommonly high road in his politicking.

While Senator Muskie was proving himself a craftsman at active politics, ex-Ambassador Gronouski hewed to his standing philosophy: Always a campaigner but never a candidate. His story in politics reads differently from that of his fellow Polish-American, yet both exemplify the modern Polish-American success story.

Gronouski rose to nationwide notice from a background of teacher, scholar, and state government administrator. A partisan Democrat all his adult life, Gronouski never has run for public office. In Wisconsin, as a militant party leader, he worked steadily to rebuild the state Democratic party from its shambles of the 1950's. In 1960, he supported Senator John F. Kennedy against all contenders for the presidential nomination in the Wisconsin primary when more established state Democratic figures hesitated or backed other candidates. Later, he pushed hard in the cause of Kennedy's election. During another election year, 1964, Gronouski again was on the stump, but, again, not in his own behalf; he gave speeches in support of President Johnson. In 1968, once more, he worked to advance Democratic leadership in the United States.

Born in the hamlet of Dunbar in northeastern Wisconsin on October 26, 1919, Gronouski grew up in Oshkosh. His father was of Polish descent; his mother, Irish. His paternal grandparents immigrated to the United States from Poznan, then under Prussian domination, in 1875. The reason, Gronouski explains, is that his grandfather, who was about twenty years old at the time, was determined, like others, to beat the Bismarck army draft. Gronouski's father, the late

John, Sr., trained as a teacher and then taught high school physics. Originally, the family name was spelled with a "w" rather than "u." When, however, the father's teaching certificate was made out to "Gronouski," this spelling stuck.

The younger Gronouski obtained his elementary and secondary schooling at a parochial school in Oshkosh and then attended the State Teachers college there. (This now is the Wisconsin State College at Oshkosh.) He transferred to the University of Wisconsin at Madison to earn degrees up to the Ph.D. in the field of economics, with a major in public finance.

After receiving his bachelor's degree in 1942, Gronouski entered the Army Air Corps as a private. Later, he served as a navigator in the Eighth Air Force and flew twenty-four combat missions in the European Theater of Operations. Shot down over the English Channel in the summer of 1944, Gronouski survived by bailing out, even though his parachute was on upside down. ("I've been lucky all my life," he says.) Discharged in October, 1945, he held the rank of first lieutenant.

Resuming his studies, Gronouski obtained his master's degree in 1947. While writing his doctoral dissertation, he held various teaching jobs, in economics, public finance, and banking. He was at the University of Maine, Roosevelt College in Chicago, and Wayne

State University, Detroit. He also pursued different research projects centered on state tax questions and administration. In 1955, he was awarded a doctorate by the University of Wisconsin.

Wisconsin, the scene of Gronouski's Democratic party climb and professional advancement also gave him a wife. In 1948, he married the former Mary Louise Metz, of Madison, a location that became their favorite American city. Two children, Stacy and Julie, comprise the family.

Gronouski won the civil service appointment as research director of the Wisconsin Department of Taxation in 1959; he also became research head of the University of Wisconsin tax impact study. A year later, Governor Gaylord Nelson (now Senator Nelson) named him Wisconsin Commissioner of Taxation. During Gronouski's term, the state initiated new tax plans and the administrative structure of the department was overhauled.

The naming of Gronouski to the office of Postmaster General partly was seen as political payment, partly as merit on grounds of administrative ability. Asked at a press conference on September 12, 1963, whether Gronouski's nationality heritage had any bearing on the appointment, President Kennedy replied: "I think Mr. Gronouski is a fine public servant. I'm glad to have him here, and I think we just happen to be fortunate that his grandparents came from Poland." In taking office, Gronouski became the only known member of any cabinet in United States history to hold an earned doctorate.

The appointment brought in letters of pride to Gronouski from Poles all over the United States and the new Postmaster General related: "They say they can point to me and tell their children they have opportunity like anyone else . . . Some have said that their children were looked down on in school before, but they aren't anymore." Gronouski recalled that while in grade school in Oshkosh he may have been on the defensive at times because he was Polish, "but I became quite an extrovert and got over it." Having achieved the status of a "symbol" to Polish-Americans, Gronouski was nudged into a closer examination and knowledge of his Polish heritage. He took up study of the Polish language, for an hour a day, five days a week, under guidance of a tutor.

At the time of his appointment, the frank-spoken administrator offered the information, when queried about his postal background: "During the 1960 presidential campaign, I licked a lot of postage stamps." His wife contributed the accessory comment: "All I can tell you is that I'm always finding letters in his pockets that he has been carrying around a couple of weeks."

When Gronouski stepped into his new job and launched steps to solve different problems, there was some apprehension, as employees watched his work pace, that he might even take the Pony Express rider off the Post Office seal in favor of something speedier and more modern. He went about changing almost everything else in the unwieldy department.

The $25,000-a-year cabinet post moved Gronouski into a vast suite in the capital Post Office department and made him the nation's biggest civilian employer with some 600,000 persons on his payroll. The department budget was almost five billion dollars a year. The new chief faced many problems: Zooming mail volume; demands for faster service and lower costs; automation; racial equality; and political patronage. As the employer of 90,000 Negroes, the largest number of any federal department, Postmaster General Gronouski committed himself to advancing equal rights and a policy of nondiscrimination.

He gained a reputation as an innovator. He slashed the Post Office deficit and wooed big mailers to make some changes; promoted the five-number ZIP system, carving the country into postal zones; and inaugurated an in-house management consultant operation, among other steps. Also, the genial pipe-smoker traveled widely to give speeches and to build good relations.

As a cabinet officer, Gronouski proved what others knew about him in other situations: While he exudes an air of rumpled relaxation, he drives himself relentlessly and expects his staff to do the same. But his

low-key appearance tends to disarm people around
him. He stands some five feet, ten inches tall, on a
frame of comfortable stockiness. His glance is as direct
as his manner, which is affable and easy. He speaks in
good-natured tones that tend to be scratchy, and conveys an engaging kind of old-shoe slackness. A crooked
stem pipe is his trademark. President Johnson characterized Gronouski as "a warm human being who
enjoys people."

In June, 1964, Gronouski made his first trip to
Poland to represent President Johnson at the annual
international trade fair at Poznan. Upon his arrival, he
delivered a short speech in his newly-learned Polish.
About his being a "newcomer" to the language, Gronouski explained: *"Lepiej pozno niz nigdy."* ("Better
late than never.") It was obvious from the applause
that his Polish listeners had no trouble understanding
him. Gronouski met the people by stretching a friendly
handshake wherever he went. As a Catholic, he attended mass at Warsaw's St. John's Cathedral where
well-wishers crowded around him. "We greet you with
our whole Polish heart!" residents of the capital
shouted to him. *"Sto lat!"* ("A hundred years!") came
the wish for long well-being.

At Poznan, Gronouski glimpsed the industrial area
from which his father's parents had come. Here he
toured the banner-bedecked fairgrounds housing ex-

hibits from more than fifty countries and met one special teen-ager, a fourteen-year-old girl who was the pen pal of his daughter, Stacy. Unfortunately, Gronouski's visit was cut short by the death of his father at the family home in Two Rivers, Wisconsin. Before leaving, he told listeners at the fairgrounds: "Polish-Americans have done very well in the United States. They may be found among our most prominent doctors, lawyers, scientists, military and naval officers, and hierarchy and clergy. They work in every field of endeavor. They have done well because they found opportunity in America and because they brought something with them. They brought a heritage of courage and faith which enabled them to join in the new way of life they found in America and to earn the respect and admiration of their fellow Americans. . . ."

In February, 1965, Gronouski was reappointed as Postmaster General after Johnson advanced from the vice-presidency to the Chief of State following the assassination of President Kennedy. But a year and a half later, President Johnson, in a surprise announcement, named Gronouski the American ambassador to Poland. It was a key post for many reasons, a foremost consideration being that Warsaw ranks as the one spot in the world where the United States and Communist China maintain regular diplomatic contact in face-to-face talks between representatives of the two countries.

As the American ambassador, Gronouski stepped into this important conference role.

Gronouski tackled Polish-American relations, his day-to-day concern, with a fast-growing knowledge of the language and strong backgrounding in the history and culture of the country. He served as a sort of roving ambassador to other East European nations in carrying out President Johnson's expressed wish to build "bridges of understanding." In late 1966 and early 1967, Gronouski is reported to have been the American contact in an attempt to work toward settlement of the Vietnam War through Polish diplomats. The affable Wisconsinite took a less rule-clad posture in foreign policy matters than some of his fellow diplomats; with his direct contact to Washington leading straight to the White House, he was in a position to handle negotiations a bit differently.

The decision of Ambassador Gronouski to leave Warsaw after two and a half years to plunge into the political fray was a difficult one; he himself commented that it was not easy to give up the post of ambassador "to such a fascinating place as Warsaw."

But he, as well as Senator Muskie, entrust the future to a comforting phrase that once applied almost exclusively to the Irish in politics. It used to be "the luck of the Irish" but, nowadays, "the luck of the Polish" has gained application, too.

Rooted in America

> "We, United States citizens of Polish birth or extraction, have found political and religious freedom and full opportunities for intellectual and material advancement; but we stand ready to give all we have, and then ourselves and our children, to uphold American honor, to defend American soil, and we shall not think our sacrifices too great a price for our liberty."

THE SUCCESS STORIES of Poles or those of Polish background in the United States are many and they stretch to widely diverse fields, from baseball to biochemistry. Immigrants found opportunity and worked hard to turn it to their advantage and to the gain of the country. As an immediate contribution, the bulk of the Polish newcomers contributed physical stamina and skill to the industrial advancement of America, in factories and foundries and mines. Brawn must be put down as a gift to the development of this nation at the time of the mass Polish immigration; it was then man-power and not so much technology that pushed forward industrial frontiers. The children of immigrants were offered the chance for complete education in America and, for the most part, they seized it. Over the years, Americans with Polish names advanced into all professions, all spheres, all societies. They advanced as different avenues in the intellectual and business world opened to them as well as to Italians, Greeks, and other nationalities. The Horatio Alger success tale of a poor boy striking it rich applied to Poles, too. The early heroes of this tale, however, were sports figures, for they cut across nationality boundaries and appealed to the wide American public.

For Poles, Stan Musial worked magic. As a baseball hero, he probably brought more sympathy, recognition, and luster to the nationality as a whole than generations of intellectuals. The son of a Polish immigrant, the St. Louis Cardinal slugger set a remarkable sports record, winning followers not just for his athletic performance but for his exemplary attitude and sportsmanship as well. When Musial retired from the playing field, he became, in 1965, adviser to the president of the United States on the nation's physical fitness. "Baseball," commented Musial, "has taught me the opportunity that America offers to any young men who want to get to the top in anything. . . ."

The story of his life began in Donora, just south of

Pittsburgh in the industrial Monongahela Valley. Musial's father, a quiet Pole named Lukasz, had come alone to America from a farm near Warsaw. The father worked in a wire mill and married a native-born American of Czech descent. The couple had six children, the fifth of whom was a boy named Stanislaus. The father called his son by the affectionate Polish "Stashu"; the name became Stanley in school and eventually "Stan" to the American public.

From the time he was eight years old, "Stashu" wanted to be a ballplayer. The first toy he remembered was a ball and when there were no extra funds to buy one, his mother fashioned one out of bits and pieces of cloth, sewn together. Young Musial played sand-lot ball in the neighborhood and worked at gymnastics under tutelage of the Polish Falcons, a Polish organization stressing athletics. He was invited to join a Class D Penn State League; here a scout for the St. Louis Cardinals spotted him and wanted to sign him up. The aspiring ballplayer was not yet seventeen and his father had to approve the agreement. The father hesitated because he felt his son ought to take advantage of the opportunity for further schooling and go to college. But Musial wanted to play ball more than anything else and, eventually, the father gave in. Later, Musial regretted, despite all his material success, not having a college education.

He went into the minor leagues and marriage at

about the same time. He married his high school sweet-heart, pretty, blond Lillian Labash, of Czech-Russian background. While Musial's prospects as a pitcher looked good at the beginning, his ability as a hitter began to emerge. In 1941, he jumped from a dead-armed pitcher in Class D ball to a major league out-fielder. His first Big League hit was a double and, from then on, he kept hitting, with some seasons better than others, and with some spectacular fielding as well. One performance caused the Chicago Cubs' manager to ex-plode: "Nobody can be that good!" Even when Musial happened to be in a slump, another manager, craggy-faced Casey Stengel, predicted to sportswriters: "You'll be looking at him a long, long while . . . ten . . . fifteen . . . maybe twenty years. He's up to stay."

At twenty-one, Musial was a member of baseball's world champions. He left baseball, but only tem-porarily, to go into the navy in 1945, eventually being assigned to a ship repair unit at Pearl Harbor. He was discharged in time to play the 1946 season. During this year, the nickname "Stan The Man" was born when journalists detected the chant every time Musial went to bat. In 1948, Musial had his biggest year yet, prac-tically taking a clean sweep of all possible major league honors. In 1956, he was awarded a first Player-of-the-Decade award, winning out over baseball greats like Joe DiMaggio, Ted Williams, and Bob Feller. Two years later, Musial became the highest-salaried player in National League history, at a whopping $100,000.

Baseball being a young man's game, Musial, in 1960, was benched and regarded as washed up. He was sure, however, he still could hit and stayed on to prove it, until the age of forty-three. When the incredible ball-player finally put away the bat and hung up his first baseman's mitt and outfielder's glove, the Cardinals permanently retired the number 6, the number Musial had worn during his entire career. At the time of his retirement in 1963, he had spent more than twenty years in the public eye as a major league ballplayer, had rewritten many of the record books, and joined the exclusive fraternity of players with 3,000 base hits. (Only seven others belong to this club.) He had re-mained popular not just with fans but, as importantly, with players, managers, and umpires. The game had given him recognition and honors, excitement and sat-isfaction, money and memories. Musial had given the game a dignity, discipline, and dedication. And he was pleased to be known as "a star without a first person complex," a team player all the way.

The sturdy six-footer managed a happy balance in temperament and attitude; his disposition, coupled with a pleasant face with apple cheeks, made him a natural for most-favored-treatment by the public. At the plate, he had a characteristic stance and used a wiggling movement to relax that became almost a trademark.

During his long career in baseball, Musial said he was conscious of "being Polish" and that "everyone knew it." He observed that he was aware of not only doing something for himself in sports but also doing something for the wider Polish community. As a youth, Musial was associated with the Polish Falcon organization. He also is a member of the Polish National Alliance.

When the American sports hero of Polish descent left the playing field, new honors accrued to him. Local baseball writers in St. Louis sponsored a testimonial dinner at which $40,000 was raised to build a statue of Musial at the riverfront stadium. In 1969, he was elected to baseball's Hall of Fame. Musial was granted a degree; Monmouth College in Illinois made him an honorary doctor of humanities. Upon retirement, Musial was named a vice-president of the St. Louis Cardinals organization. From 1965 to 1967, Musial promoted youth and adult fitness as adviser to President Johnson on the nation's physical fitness. He resigned from the national office to become general manager, in 1967, of the Cardinals ball team, a job entailing very active duties. In St. Louis, where Musial and his family make their home, he is also a well-known restaurateur and a bank director.

As early as the 1930's, young Americans of Polish descent won attention and acclaim for their sports ability. The *Detroit News*, for example, in 1934 ran a story with the headline: "Sons of Poland Set Athletic Pace Here." The rosters of baseball, football, and basketball teams already were studded with Polish names. The Notre Dame football coach, Knute Rockne, summarized the development nicely when he commented, during recruitment of players: "It's a cinch when I can't pronounce 'em, they're good."

Today, what newspaper reader is not aware of the outstanding career of Carl Yastrzemski, the Boston Red Sox outfielder named the American League's most valuable player in 1967? Other names in baseball indicating Polish background come quickly to mind, names like Ted Kluszewski, Ray Jablonski, and Rip (Eldon) Repulski. The all-time great, Al Simmons (really Aloysius Szymanski) was one of the sport's greatest hitters and an early inspiration to all hopeful Polish-American athletes. In football, the career of Casimir John Myslinski of West Point, the "Steel-worker's Boy," commanded national attention in 1943. And who has not read or heard of such a football hero as Alexander (the Great) Wojciechowicz (Wojie, for short)? A tackler and blocker who lasted thirteen years in the National Football League, he belongs to the Pro Football Hall of Fame. The sports list of stars of Polish background is both numerous and glittering. Certainly American sports fans can testify to the influence of the Polish-Americans in many different athletic fields.

More and more, Polish immigrants and their successive generations are becoming established in the United States, and in academic circles of other countries, as scholars and scientists. This recognition has come more slowly, and partly has been geared to the American opportunities for extended education offered the children of immigrants who arrived in the mass waves from Poland. Politics and business, science and mathematics, philosophy and logic, music and arts, education and law, religion and sociology—all these represent newer fields of achievement for the Pole or American of Polish descent in the United States. In the discipline of higher mathematics alone, more than fifty professors and instructors of Polish nationality are teaching at American universities. This represents a field in which Poles have been famous for decades, and former members of the Warsaw mathematics group now sit, as Polish-Americans, in the National Academy of Science in the United States.

A lack of space and a scarcity of materials on prominent Polish-Americans make it impossible to offer any complete or authoritative list, but scientists and scholars have been compiled in cooperation with the Polish Institute of Arts and Sciences. Stanislaw M. Ulam, currently a mathematics professor at the University of Colorado, played a leading role in developing the mathematics necessary to calculate the thermonuclear hydrogen reaction in the development of the H-bomb by the United States. Other notables are: Antoni Zygmund, of the University of Chicago, who helped to establish a real "school" of mathematics on the American educational scene after World War II; Alfred Tarski, outstanding mathematician, logician, and philosopher at the University of California at Berkeley; and additional mathematician-educators like Adam Kac, of Rockefeller University in New York; Samuel Eilenberg, of Columbia University; Jerzy Neyman, mathematical statistician, emeritus professor at Berkeley.

In other scientific disciplines, these names must be mentioned: Hilary Koprowski, director of the Wistar Institute of Anatomy and Biology at the University of Pennsylvania; Stanislaw Mrozowski, chairman of the physics department at the University of Buffalo and president of the Polish Institute of Arts and Sciences; Michael Laskowski, American Cancer Society life research professor and head of the laboratory of enzymology at Roswell Park Memorial Institute, Buffalo, New York, and his son, Michael, Jr., head of the biochemistry division at Purdue University, Lafayette, Indiana; Emil Konopinski, professor of physics at the University of Indiana at Bloomington, an expert in nuclear physics, along with the late Jerzy Sawicki, nuclear physicist who taught at Princeton and Berkeley.

Widely known as a specialist on problems and policies of Communism and the Communist-dominated world, Zbigniew Brzezinski served for eighteen months on the State Department's Policy Planning Council. Presently, he is professor of government and director of the Research Institute on Communist Affairs at Columbia University. A political scientist and author, Wladyslaw Kulski, heads the department of political science at Duke University, Durham, North Carolina, and M. K. Dziewanowski has been professor of East European history at Boston College and Harvard. In the field of history, Oscar Halecki holds distinguished rank and taught at various universities, including Vassar College, Fordham University, and Columbia University. He was a founder and remains an honorary president of the Polish Institute of Arts and Sciences.

Some scholars gave extraordinarily original pioneer effort in various fields; Florian Znaniecki, sociologist, compiled with William Thomas a four-volume work on *The Polish Peasant in Europe and America* that is recognized as a classic; Alfred Korzybski devised a new system of semantics and has been called the founder of modern semantics; Bronislaw Malinowski, anthropologist, introduced the approach known as "function-alism" to his discipline.

Waclaw Lednicki, an authority on Slavic literature, headed the department of Slavic literature and languages at the University of California at Berkeley before his recent death. He wrote prolifically and his publications included seventeen books. Wiktor Weintraub teaches Slavic literature at Harvard University and Ludwig Krzyzanowski is at New York University. Edmund Zawacki, a foremost expert in Slavic languages and literature long has been identified with the University of Wisconsin, Madison. The brilliant author of *The Captive Mind* and other works, Czeslaw Milosz, also teaches literature at Berkeley. Another author of note is Jozef Wittlin, poet, essayist, and novelist, whose book *Salt of the Earth* took an award from the American Academy of Arts and Letters.

The technical sciences list names like Thaddeus Sedzimir, responsible for important innovations in steel processing; Frank Piasecki, who helped to pioneer the development of the helicopter; and Felix Pawlowski, specialist who contributed to aeronautics engineering.

Economist Paul Rosenstein-Rodan formerly headed the economic department of the International Bank for Reconstruction and Development and now teaches at the Massachusetts Institute of Technology.

The Polish "dean" of Congress is Clement J. Zablocki, of Milwaukee, Wisconsin; others on the list of the House of Representatives include Daniel Rostenkowski, John Kluczynski and Roman Pucinski of Chicago; Alvin O'Konski, of Mercer, Wisconsin; Thaddeus Dulski, of Buffalo, New York; Bernard Grabowski, of Bristol, Connecticut; and Edward J. Derwinski, of South Holland, Illinois. At community and state levels, elected officials of Polish ancestry fill a variety of offices from mayor to state legislative representatives.

Jerzy Soltan teaches architecture and urban design at the Graduate School of Design at Harvard; another recognized name in architecture is Wladyslaw Biernacki-Poray, who designed the American-donated children's hospital outside Cracow, Poland. W. T. Benda was famous as a mask-maker, Henry Arctowski as an Arctic explorer. Korczak Ziolkowski, a sculptor of rock, is carving a massive Indian monument in South Dakota to rival Mount Rushmore.

Polish-American clergymen have been advancing to higher titles within the Catholic Church and, in 1967, Archbishop John Krol of Philadelphia was among four new American cardinals named by Pope Paul VI. Bishops and other ranking clergy in many states bear Polish names.

The performing arts offer a long list of distinguished Polish-American artists. Here are a few: Wanda

Landowska, pianist and harpsichordist; Mieczyslaw Horszowski and Josef Hofmann, and Ruth Slenczynska, pianists; Marcella Sembrich-Kochanska, Jan Kiepura, and Edward and Jan De Reszke, opera singers. Among musical conductors, there are many respected names —Artur Rodzinski, Leopold Stokowski, and Stanislaw Skrowaczewski, to mention the best known.

In the glamor world of film-making, Carole Landis, Gilda Gray (the "shimmy" girl), and Pola Negri have gained celebrity status over the years.

As in previous generations, Poles still are contributing outstanding fighters for freedom. Colonel Francis Gabreski, America's top living air ace, only recently retired after twenty-seven years of service. He is credited with more than thirty-seven enemy aircraft during World War II and the Korean War. Recently, a Vietnam Medal of Honor winner was Major Robert Modrzejewski, United States Marine Corps.

Can we doubt, in the light of the group and individual accomplishments of Poles in America, that they really have become rooted? Through contributions of brawn and brain, they have become part of the vast, diverse, and powerful American nation and society. They have helped to build a strong America by giving it their energy, talent, love, and loyalty, along with the winged seed of their heritage evident in songs, dances, arts, foods, crafts, culture. Devotion to country runs very deep in Poles. No one Polish group has spoken of this devotion more dramatically than Milwaukee Poles who, during World War I, proclaimed:

"We, United States citizens of Polish birth or extraction, representing fully one-fifth of the half million population of Milwaukee county, in this solemn hour proudly give testimonial of the undying love and undivided loyalty which we bear to our beloved country . . .

"We have found political and religious freedom and full opportunities for intellectual and material advancement; but we stand ready to give all we have, and then ourselves and our children, to uphold American honor, to defend American soil, and we shall not think our sacrifices too great a price for our liberty."

This was a resolution adopted in 1917 at a mass meeting of Polish-American citizens in Milwaukee.

During another dark day in American history—the war days of 1944—Milwaukee launched an event which, possibly, best of all shows the variety and richness of the plural ethnic backgrounds that give strength and vividness to America's composite character. This is the annual Holiday Folk Fair begun by the enterprising International Institute of Milwaukee County in cooperation with a host of nationality groups. The 1944 fair enlisted fourteen nationalities, the Poles among them, and opened its doors to some

3,000 visitors who braved a snowstorm to tour the fair. It consisted of a costume parade, troubadour musicians, group exhibits, and food stands having an international flavor. The fair was heralded as "an ideal world in miniature, a microcosm symbolizing the happiest aspects of yesterday's world and the brightest hopes of tomorrow."

From that start, this multinationality event now enrolls some sixty-five ethnic groups and an attendance reaching some 65,000. The story of America's immigrant groups continues to be told in song, costume, and dance, foods and exhibits. The aim remains as compelling as ever: To have all nationalities meet on a common ground in promoting knowledge, friendship, and cooperation. Each ethnic group teaches and shares its joys and arts and history. The occasion ideally exemplifies the spirit of scores of nationalities, the Poles prominent among them, and spontaneously presents what has emerged as the pattern of greatness for the United States.

Bibliography

POLISH BACKGROUND

Benet, Sula. *Song, Dance and Customs of Peasant Poland*. New York: Roy, 1951.

Dyboski, Roman. (Edited by Ludwik Kryzanowski.) *Poland in World Civilization*. New York: Barrett, 1950.

Gieysztor, Alexander and others (editors). *A Thousand Years of Polish History*. Warsaw: Polonia, 1959.

Halecki, Oscar. *A History of Poland*. New York: Roy, 1956.

Lednicki, Waclaw. *Life and Culture of Poland*. New York: Roy, 1944.

Mizwa, Stephen (editor). *Great Men and Women of Poland*. New York: Macmillan, 1941.

Reddaway, W. F. and others (editors). *The Cambridge History of Poland*. New York: Cambridge University Press, 1941.

Uminski, Sigmund. *Poland's Contribution to the World's Civilization*. New York: Polish-American Press, 1942.

Van Norman, Louis. *Poland, the Knight Among Nations*. New York: Fleming Revell, 1907.

Wlosszewski, Stefan. *History of Polish-American Culture*. Trenton, N.J.: White Eagle, 1946.

Wszelaki, Jan (editor). "John F. Kennedy and Poland." New York: Auspices of the Polish Institute of Arts and Sciences, 1964.

IMMIGRATION HISTORY

Adamic, Louis. *A Nation of Nations*. New York: Harper & Brothers, 1945.

———. *Two-Way Passage*. New York: Harper & Brothers, 1941.

Borun, Thaddeus (compiler). *We, The Milwaukee Poles: 1846-1946.* Milwaukee: Nowiny Publishers, 1946.

Brown, Francis, and Roncek, Joseph. *One America.* New York: Prentice-Hall, 1937.

Chandler, Alvin Duke. "The Poles at Jamestown." *The Polish Review,* Vol. II, No. 4.

Dziob, Francis W. and others (compilers). "Jamestown: Pioneers from Poland." Published by the Polish American Congress for the 350th Anniversary of Poles landing in Jamestown. Chicago: Alliance Printers & Publishers, 1958.

Gebert, Boleslaw. *Pierwsi Polacy w Stanach Zjednoczonych.* Warsaw: Polonia, 1958.

Haiman, Miecislaus. *Polish Past in America (1608-1865).* Chicago: Polish Roman Catholic Union Archives & Museum, 1939.

Janta, Alexander. "Barriers into Bridges: Notes on the Problem of Polish Culture in America." *The Polish Review,* Vol. II, No. 2-3, 1957.

Kusielewicz, Eugene. "The Poles Among Us." *Extension* Magazine, August, 1966.

Lednicki, Waclaw. "The Role of the Polish Intellectual in America." *The Polish Review.*

Lerski, Jerzy. *A Polish Chapter in Jacksonian America: The United States and the Polish Exiles of 1831.* Madison: University of Wisconsin Press, 1958.

Mondello, Salvatore. "America's Polish Heritage as Viewed by Miecislaus Haiman and the Periodical Press." *The Polish Review,* Vol. VI, No. 1-2, 1959.

Starczewska, Maria. "Historical Geography of the Oldest Polish Settlement in the United States." *The Polish Review,* Vol. XII, No. 2, 1967.

Thomas, William, and Znaniecki, Florian. *The Polish Peasant in Europe and America.* London: Dover, 1958.

Wachtl, Karol. *Polonja w Ameryce.* Philadelphia: Polish Star Publishers, 1944.

Wankowicz, Melchior. *Polacy i Ameryka.* Under auspices of the Poets' and Painters' Organization of England. Newton: Montgomeryshire Printers, 1954.

Wieczerzak, Joseph. *A Polish Chapter in Civil War America.* New York: Twayne, 1967.

Wood, Arthur Evans. *Hamtramck Then and Now*. New York: Book-man Associates, 1955.

Wytrwal, Joseph. *America's Polish Heritage: A Social History of the Poles in the United States*. Detroit: Endurance Press, 1961.

PULASKI

Adams, Dorothy. *Cavalry Hero: Casimir Pulaski*. New York: Kenedy, 1957.

Haiman, Miecislaus. *Poland and the American Revolutionary War*. Chicago: Polish Roman Catholic Union Archives and Museum, 1932.

Malone, Dumas (editor). *Dictionary of American Biography*. Auspices of the American Council of Learned Societies. London: Oxford University Press; New York: Scribner's, 1928.

KOSCIUSZKO

Gardner, Monica. *Kosciuszko*. London: Allen, 1920.

Haiman, Miecislaus. "Kosciuszko in the American Revolution." Polish Institute of Arts and Sciences, Series No. 4. New York: Herald Square Press, 1943.

Korzon, Tadeusz. *Kim i Czem Byl Kosciuszko*. Warsaw and Cracow: Gebethner, 1907.

Mizwa, Stephen. *Tadeusz Kosciuszko*. An address by the president of the Kosciuszko Foundation, October 21, 1967, published in pamphlet form. Brooklyn: Czas Publishers.

Tatarinoff, Adele. *Tadeusz Kosciuszko 1746-1817*. Solothurn, Switzerland: Gassmann AG, 1967. A German language publication.

SADOWSKI

Haiman, Miecislaus. *Polish Pioneers of Virginia and Kentucky*. (Notes on genealogy of the Sadowski family by A. Clay Sanduski). Chicago: Polish Roman Catholic Union Archives and Museum, 1937.

————. *Polish Pioneers of Pennsylvania*. Chicago: Polish Roman Catholic Union Archives and Museum, 1941.

Pinkowski, Edward. "Anthony Sadowski: Polish Pioneer." Pamphlet published by Sadowski Memorial Committee, Philadelphia, Pa., 1966.

MODJESKA

Coleman, Arthur P. and Marion M. *Wanderers Twain*. Cheshire, Conn.: Cherry Hill Books, 1964.

Coleman, Marion M. "Source Materials on Modjeska's First Appearance on the American Stage." *Books and Things,* Winter 1964-Spring 1965. Cheshire, Conn.: Cherry Hill Books.

Coleman, Marion M. "A Polish Play for Modjeska." *Polish-American Studies,* January-June, 1965.

Modjeska, Helena. *Memories and Impressions*. New York: Macmillan, 1910.

Terlecki, Tymon. *Pani Helena*. London: Veritas Foundation Press, 1962. Published in Polish.

PADEREWSKI

Gronowicz, Antoni. *Paderewski: Pianist and Patriot*. New York: Nelson, 1944. Translated from the Polish.

Hume, Ruth and Paul. *The Lion of Poland*. New York: Hawthorn, 1962.

Jarocinski, Stefan (editor). *Polish Music*. Warsaw: Polish Scientific Publishers, 1965.

Paderewski, Ignace Jan and Lawton, Mary. *The Paderewski Memoirs*. New York: Scribner's, 1939.

Phillips, Charles. *Paderewski: The Story of a Modern Immortal*. New York: Macmillan, 1934.

Strakacz, Aniela. *Paderewski as I Knew Him*. New Brunswick: Rutgers University Press, 1949.

FUNK

Harrow, Benjamin. *Casimir Funk: Pioneer in Vitamins and Hormones*. New York: Dodd, Mead, 1955.

NOWICKI

Evenson, Norma. *Chandigarh*. University of California Press, 1966.

Mumford, Lewis. "The Life, the Teaching and the Architecture of Matthew Nowicki." *Architectural Record*. Four articles, June through September, 1954.

RUBINSTEIN

Sargeant, Winthrop. *Geniuses, Goddesses & People.* New York: Dutton, 1949.

Schonberg, Harold. "The Rubinstein Touch, Untouched at 75." *The New York Times Magazine,* January 26, 1954.

Time Magazine. "Pianists: The Undeniable Romantic." February 25, 1966.

Wechsberg, Joseph. "Profiles: Metamorphosis." *The New Yorker.* November, 1958.

GRONOUSKI

Business Week. "Can He Really Put Zip in the Mails?" June 19, 1965.

Current Biography. January, 1966.

The Milwaukee Journal. Series of articles on first trip to Poland by Postmaster-General Gronouski by Laura Pilarski, June 5-8, 1964.

The Milwaukee Journal. "Gronouski Welds China Link," by John Reddin, November 29, 1967.

Newsweek. "Hyphenated General." September 23, 1963.

The New York Times. "Outspoken Postal Chief." February 16, 1965.

MUSKIE

Current Biography. 1955.

Look Magazine. "Miracle Man from Maine." November 25, 1958.

Newsweek. "The Making of a Running Mate." September 9, 1968.

———. "The Making of the Veep." October 7, 1968.

The New York Times. "Big Democrat from G.O.P. Maine." August 30, 1968.

———. "When in Doubt, Vote for Muskie!" by James Reston, September 29, 1968.

Time Magazine. "Humphrey's Polish Yankee." September 6, 1968.

MUSIAL

Broeg, Bob. *Stan Musial: "The Man's" Own Story* (as told to Bob Broeg). Garden City: Doubleday, 1964.

Index

ABOUT THE AUTHOR

LAURA PILARSKI was born in Niagara Falls, New York, where her parents, who had immigrated separately from Poland, met and married. After graduation from Syracuse University where she was elected to Phi Beta Kappa, she joined the staff of *The Milwaukee Journal* and wrote widely of the community's Polish population.

Miss Pilarski made her first trip to Poland in 1956 with the first postwar group of Wisconsin Poles to travel there. This resulted in a series of articles entitled "This is Poland." She again visited the country in 1958 as leader of a group of young people under the Experiment in International Living program. Later, she returned to Europe to tour and write, and went to Warsaw for a longer stay, further studying the language and culture while continuing to furnish articles on Polish themes for various newspapers and magazines in the United States.

At present Miss Pilarski lives in Zurich, Switzerland, where she is chief correspondent for McGraw-Hill World News Service. She is a member of the Overseas Press Club and the Foreign Press Association of Switzerland.